双双中文教材 (15)
Chinese Language and Culture Course

中國文學欣賞 *Appreciation of Chinese Literature*

王雙雙　編著

北京大學出版社
PEKING UNIVERSITY PRESS

圖書在版編目（CIP）數據

中國文學欣賞：繁體版／王雙雙編著．—北京：北京大學出版社，2008.10
（雙雙中文教材・15）

ISBN 978-7-301-14204-2

Ⅰ.中… Ⅱ.王… Ⅲ.漢語－對外漢語教學－教材 Ⅳ.H195.4

中國版本圖書館CIP數據核字（2008）第134732號

書　　　　名：	中國文學欣賞
著作責任者：	王雙雙 編著
英 文 翻 譯：	王亦兵 熊文華
封 面 圖 案：	劉　藝
責 任 編 輯：	孫　嫻
標 準 書 號：	ISBN 978-7-301-14204-2／H・2057
出 版 發 行：	北京大學出版社
地　　　　址：	北京市海淀區成府路205號　100871
網　　　　址：	http://www.pup.cn
電　　　　話：	郵購部 62752015　發行部 62750672　編輯部 62752028　出版部 62754962
電 子 信 箱：	zpup@pup.pku.edu.cn
印 刷 者：	北京大學印刷廠
經 銷 者：	新華書店
	889毫米×1194毫米　16開本　11印張　189千字
	2008年10月第1版　　2008年10月第1次印刷
定　　　　價：	100.00元（含課本、練習冊和CD-ROM一張）

未經許可，不得以任何方式複製或抄襲本書之部分或全部內容。
版權所有，侵權必究
舉報電話：010-62752024
電子信箱：fd@pup.pku.edu.cn

前 言

　　《雙雙中文教材》是一套專門為海外青少年編寫的中文課本，是我在美國八年的中文教學實踐基礎上編寫成的。在介紹這套教材之前，請讀一首小詩：

> 一双神奇的手，
> 推开一扇窗。
> 一条神奇的路，
> 通向灿烂的中华文化。
>
> 　　　　鮑凱文　鮑維江
> 　　　　1998年

　　鮑維江和鮑凱文姐弟倆是美國生美國長的孩子，也是我的學生。1998年冬，他們送給我的新年賀卡上的小詩，深深地打動了我的心。我把這首詩看成我文化教學的回聲。我要傳達給海外每位中文老師：我教給他們（學生）中國文化，他們思考了、接受了、回應了。這條路走通了！

　　語言是交際的工具，更是一種文化和一種生活方式，所以學習中文也就離不開中華文化的學習。漢字是一種古老的象形文字，她從遠古走來，帶有大量的文化信息，但學起來並不容易。使學生增強興趣、減小難度，走出苦學漢字的怪圈，走進領悟中華文化的花園，是我編寫這套教材的初衷。

　　學生不論大小，天生都有求知的慾望，都有欣賞文化美的追求。中華文化本身是魅力十足的。把這宏大而玄妙的文化，深入淺出地，有聲有色地介紹出來，讓這迷人的文化如涓涓細流，一點一滴地滲入學生們的心田，使學生們逐步體味中國文化，是我編寫這套教材的目的。

　　為此我將漢字的學習放入文化介紹的流程之中同步進行，讓同學們在學中國地理的同時，學習漢字；在學中國歷史的同時，學習漢字；在學中國哲學的同時，學習漢字；在學中國科普文選的同時，學習漢字……

　　這樣的一種中文學習，知識性強，趣味性強；老師易教，學生易學。當學生們合上書本時，他們的眼前是中國的大好河山，是中國五千年的歷史和妙不可言的哲學思維，是奔騰的現代中國……

　　總之，他們瞭解了中華文化，就會探索這片土地，熱愛這片土地，就會與中國結下情緣。

　　最後我要衷心地感謝所有熱情支持和幫助我編寫教材的老師、家長、學生、朋友和家人，特別是老同學唐玲教授、何茜老師、我姐姐王欣欣編審及我女兒Uta Guo年復一年的鼎力相助。可以說這套教材是大家努力的結果。

王雙雙

說 明

　　《雙雙中文教材》是一套專門為海外學生編寫的中文教材。它是由美國加州王雙雙老師和中國專家學者共同努力，在海外多年的實踐中編寫出來的。全書共20冊，識字量2500個，包括了從識字、拼音、句型、短文的學習，到初步的較系統的中國文化的學習。教材大體介紹了中國地理、歷史、哲學等方面的豐富內容，突出了中國文化的魅力。課本知識面廣，趣味性強，深入淺出，易教易學。

　　這套教材體系完整、構架靈活、使用面廣。學生可以從零起點開始，一直學完全部課程20冊；也可以將後11冊（10~20冊）的九個文化專題和第五冊（漢語拼音）單獨使用，這樣便於開設中國哲學、地理、歷史等專門課程以及假期班、短期中國文化班、拼音速成班的高中和大學使用，符合了美國AP中文課程的目標和基本要求。

　　本書是《雙雙中文教材》的第十五冊。適用於已完成前十四冊的學習，對中國文化有了基本瞭解，文字上也相對扎實，掌握1000個以上漢字的學生使用。課文選取各具風格的古典名著和現代作品的章節、片斷改編而成，內容有趣、觀點新穎。每課的篇幅都在1000~1500字左右，詞彙量開始加大。通過學習，學生們可以初步接觸到一些中國古典、現代的文學作品，為今後大量閱讀打下良好的基礎。

編者

課程設置

一年級	中文課本（第一冊）	中文課本（第二冊）	中文課本（第三冊）
二年級	中文課本（第四冊）	中文課本（第五冊）	中文課本（第六冊）
三年級	中文課本（第七冊）	中文課本（第八冊）	中文課本（第九冊）
四年級	中國成語故事	中國地理常識	
五年級	中國古代故事	中國神話傳說	
六年級	中國古代科學技術	中國文學欣賞	
七年級	中國詩歌欣賞	中文科普閱讀	
八年級	中國古代哲學	中國歷史（上）	
九年級	中國歷史（下）	小說閱讀，中文SAT II	
十年級	中文SAT II（強化班）	小說閱讀，中文SAT II 考試	

目　錄

第一課　　武松打虎……………………………………1

第二課　　女兒國………………………………………10

第三課　　草船借箭……………………………………17

第四課　　孫悟空三打白骨精…………………………27

第五課　　雞毛信………………………………………39

第六課　　木蘭辭………………………………………49

第七課　　將相和………………………………………57

第八課　　考試…………………………………………67

第九課　　《臥虎藏龍》選段…………………………78

第十課　　黛玉與寶玉…………………………………90

生字表……………………………………………………101

生詞表……………………………………………………105

第一課

武松打虎

　　武松是一位梁山好漢。有一次他回家，路上要經過一座大山。來到山前，武松看見一個酒店。他走得又累又渴，就進去買酒喝。他一口氣喝了三大碗，喝完了還要求店家給他添酒，店家卻不肯添。武松問："為什麼不給我添酒？"店家說："這種酒叫做'三碗不過岡'，意思是說，人喝了三碗之後就會醉倒。"武松聽了哈哈大笑，說："我喝酒是海量，從來沒醉過。"店家又說："前面的山叫景陽岡。最近岡上出了一隻老虎，已經把好幾個人吃掉了。你酒喝多了，可不能上山了。"武松不信，只管要酒，店家只好不斷地給他倒酒。結果武松一共喝了十八碗。喝完酒，武松不聽店家的勸告，提著一根棍子就上山去了。

　　來到山腳下，他看見一張官府的佈告，纔知道真的有老虎。他想：我有棍子，怕什麼虎！就繼續往前走。這時，太陽已經落山了。武松覺得渾身熱起來，頭也有些暈了，原來他酒喝得太多了。他看見路邊有一塊大石頭正好可以躺下休息，就把棍子放在一邊，往石頭上一躺，睡著了。

　　忽然，颳起一陣大風，把武松驚醒了。風剛吹過，一隻兇猛

的大老虎就從樹林裏撲了出來。武松"啊呀"一聲，從大石頭上翻身跳起，這一下把他的酒也嚇醒了。只見老虎瞪著兩隻眼睛向武松撲來。武松轉身一閃，就閃到了老虎的背後，老虎撲了一個空。老虎連撲了兩下都沒有撲著，氣得大吼一聲，聲音好像打雷一樣。它又把尾巴豎起來向武松一掃。武松再一閃，又躲開了。趁著老虎還沒轉過身來，武松連忙抓起棍子，用盡全身的力氣，掄起來向下打去。沒想到武松打得太急了，一下子打到一棵樹上，棍子斷成了兩截。這時，老虎轉過身，又向武松撲過來，武松往後一跳，老虎正好撲到武松的眼前。武松急忙扔下棍子，跳上前去，死死地抓住老虎的頭，用盡所有的力氣往下按。

王金泰 畫

老虎被武松緊緊地按在地上，雖然使勁掙扎，但就是起不來，它就用兩隻爪子在地上亂抓，抓著抓著，把地挖出了一個坑。武松雙手按住老虎的同時，又抬起腳往老虎的頭上亂踢。老虎漸漸沒有力氣了。武松舉起右手，掄起鐵錘般的拳頭，照著老虎的頭使勁地打，打了幾十下，老虎就一點兒也不動了。

武松獨自一人赤手空拳打死老虎的事情很快就傳開了，大家都爭先恐後地來看打虎的英雄。官府給了他一些賞錢，他把這些錢都分給了近來一直辛苦打虎的獵人們。從此，他更受大家的敬重了。

（根據施耐庵、羅貫中著《水滸傳》選段改編）

作品簡介

《水滸傳》是中國第一部以白話文寫出的長篇小說，作者施耐庵是元朝末年明朝初年的人。《水滸傳》、《三國演義》、《西遊記》和《紅樓夢》被稱為"中國古典四大名著"。

《水滸傳》講的是梁山一百零八個好漢的故事。書中人物個性鮮明，活躍生動。他們都愛打抱不平，反對貪官，被逼上梁山，起義造反。他們重朋友、輕生死、講義氣的行為，體現了當時中國大眾的道德觀念。

《水滸傳》故事曲折、語言生動，被翻譯成多種文字。其中一種英文版的書名為 All Men Are Brothers。

生詞

liáng shān 梁山	Liangshan (*name of a Mountain*)	liǎng jié 兩截	two parts
jiǔ diàn 酒店	inn; tavern	shǐ jìn 使勁	exert all of one's strength
jǐng yánggāng 景陽岡	Jingyang Ridge (*of a hill*)	zhēng zhá 掙扎	struggle
zuì 醉	drunk	tī 踢	kick
quàn gào 勸告	advice	tiě chuí 鐵錘	hammer
bù gào 佈告	bulletin; notice	quán tou 拳頭	fist
zhèng hǎo 正好	by chance	chì shǒu kōng quán 赤手空拳	barehanded
hǒu 吼	roar	zhēng xiān kǒng hòu 爭先恐後	compete with each other
shù 豎	erect; upright		over something
chèn zhe 趁著	take advantage of	shǎngqián 賞錢	monetary reward
lūn 掄	swing		

聽寫

酒店　佈告　趁著　踢　拳頭　使勁　豎　正好

爭先恐後　*鐵錘　掙扎

注: 標有*號的字詞為選做題,後同。

比一比

店 { 飯店 / 旅店 / 書店 / 理髮店 / 小吃店

賞 { 賞錢 / 欣賞

{ 錘（鐵錘）/ 睡（睡覺）

{ 掙（掙扎）/ 爭（爭先恐後）

詞語運用

趁著

趁著天還沒黑，你趕快回家吧。

趁著飯還熱，趕快吃吧。

趁著爸爸有假期，咱們全家去黃石公園旅遊吧。

爭先恐後

同學們爭先恐後地報名參加學校的運動會。

最近要舉行世界杯足球賽，人們都爭先恐後地買票(piào)觀看。

近義詞

使勁——盡力——用力　　　　好漢——英雄

反義詞

使勁——省力　　　　竪——橫

多音字

傳 chuán
傳開 chuán

傳 zhuàn
水滸傳 hǔ zhuàn

回答問題

1. ｛武松聽了大笑。
   ｛武松聽了哈哈大笑。

   哪一句更生動？為什麼？

2. ｛只見老虎瞪著兩隻眼睛向武松撲過來。
   ｛老虎連撲了兩下都沒撲著，氣得大吼一聲，聲音好像打雷一樣。

   這兩句話中哪些詞語寫出了老虎的兇猛？

詞語解釋

赤手空拳——沒有使用任何武器，空著手打鬥。

爭先恐後——爭著向前，生怕落後。

相配詞連線

掄起	腳
不聽	力氣
抬起	拳頭
用盡	勸告

Lesson One

Wu Song Fighting with Tiger

Wu Song was a hero in Liangshan. One day, on his way home, he passed an inn at the foot of a mountain. Having journeyed a long way, he felt tired and thirsty and so he entered the inn to order some wine. He drank three large bowls of wine and asked for more. But the innkeeper refused to serve him. Wu Song asked him why and the innkeeper replied, "The wine you had is named 'Three Bowls and You Can't Pass the Ridge,' which means that those who have drunk three bowls of it would become too drunk to go on with their journey." Wu Song laughed at his words and said, "I can drink a lot and I have never gotten drunk before." The innkeeper said, "The mountain ahead is called the Jingyang Ridge. A tiger there has already devoured several people. You've had too much to drink and it will be dangerous for you. Don't go up the mountain." However, Wu Song refused to believe him and insisted that the innkeeper bring him more wine. The innkeeper had no other choice but to oblige. In the end, Wu Song drank a total of 18 bowls of wine. He then took his stick and headed toward the mountain despite the innkeeper's warning.

Upon reaching the foot of the mountain, he saw an official announcement and realized that what the innkeeper said was true. But he thought, "I have a stick. Why should I be afraid of a tiger?" With that, Wu Song continued his journey. By then, the sun had already set. Due to having too much to drink, Wu Song began to feel hot and dizzy. He saw a large boulder where he could lie down and rest, so he put his stick aside, crawled onto the boulder, and fell asleep.

Suddenly, a strong gust of wind woke him up. He saw a huge ferocious tiger charging at him from out of the forest. Wu Song shouted and jumped down from the boulder immediately. The sudden appearance of the tiger had shaken him out of his stupor. With its eyes on him, the tiger pounced at Wu Song who dodged and went round to its back. Having failed in its first attempt, the tiger launched two more assaults but failed again both times. The angry tiger let out a roar that was as loud as thunder. It raised its tail high and swept at Wu Song. Wu Song managed to evade the animal again. While the tiger's back was not yet turned, he immediately grabbed his stick and struck at the animal with all his strength. Unfortunately, in his haste, the stick hit a tree and broke into two parts. The tiger turned around and pounced at Wu Song again. Wu Song jumped back and the tiger landed just in front of him. Quickly discarding the broken stick, Wu Song jumped up and grabbed the tiger by its head, pushing it down to the ground with all his might.

Under Wu Song's tight grip, the tiger could not free itself despite its struggles. It dug at the ground with its two front paws, making a deep hole. Wu Song held the animal down with his two hands while kicking hard at its head. The tiger finally ran out of strength. Raising his right fist, Wu Song struck its head several dozen times until the tiger gradually became motionless.

The story of Wu Song slaying a tiger with his bare hands spread far and wide. People rushed to see the hero who had killed the tiger. The local official rewarded him with cash but Wu Song gave the money to the hunters who had a hard time hunting for the tiger. From then on, Wu Song became even more popular and gained the people's respect.

(Excerpted and Abbreviated from *Outlaws of the Marsh*)

第二課

女兒國

唐朝有個書生叫唐敖(áo)，他和朋友林之洋、多九公三個人一起到海外去經商。

他們在茫茫大海上航行了很久。一天，他們看到一片陸地，上岸以後，發現這裏無論種地的、做工的還是做買賣的都是女人。她們說話都粗聲大氣的，還穿著男人的衣服，唐敖他們覺得非常奇怪。三個人來到一家客店，一個穿著男人衣服的女人出來歡迎他們，說自己就是這家客店的老闆。她回頭招呼手下人來幫忙，出來的是一個穿著女人衣服的男人。他雖然身材很高大，臉上還長著鬍子，可是走起路來扭扭捏捏的，說話也細聲細氣的，臉上還擦著香粉和胭脂呢！唐敖他們覺得這真是稀奇古怪，彆扭極了。

　　漸漸地，唐敖他們纔明白，這個地方叫女兒國，女人是管理國家大事的，在外做事的也都是女人，男人反而在家裏做家務。唐敖他們在街上做了幾天買賣，有人來對他們說："你們的首飾和化妝品非常好，我們國王想買些給宮'女'們用，你們進宮去談談價錢吧。"

　　不料進宮後，女國王一見到他們，就看上了林之洋，不由分說就封了林之洋做"娘娘"。馬上，一大群宮"女"就來給林之洋換衣服、戴花、擦胭脂；有人見他沒有扎耳朵眼兒，拿起針就替他扎了兩個，疼得他直叫；還有人看到他沒有纏足，就拿來一根布條，把他的兩隻腳緊緊地纏了起來，這下林之洋走路都要人扶著纔行。林之洋覺得纏足太痛苦了，就自己把布條拆下來，把腳放開了。國王知道了，非常生氣地說："你這樣不守規矩，怎麼行呢？我得教訓教訓你。"於是，她叫人把林之洋狠狠地打了一頓。不管他怎麼哀求，國王還是下令把他關起來，準備過幾天就與他結婚。

　　唐敖和多九公回到客店，左思右想，想了好久，纔想出了一個辦法：結婚以前，新娘是不能在丈夫家住的。於是他們就對國王說："林之洋必須回客店住。等結婚的時候，您再派人來接他進宮吧。"國王答應了並把林之洋放了回來，但是在客店周圍派了許多人看守著。

　　晚上，趁著夜色，唐敖和多九公背著渾身是傷的林之洋，躲

過了國王的衛兵,急急忙忙地跑出客店,上船逃離了這個古怪的女兒國。

(根據李汝珍著《鏡花緣》選段改編)

作品簡介

《鏡花緣》是清代小說家李汝珍寫的一部思想開放、想象新奇的小說。故事講述了武則天當皇帝時,一個叫唐敖的書生和朋友林之洋、多九公出海經商過程中的神奇見聞。

生詞

經商 jīng shāng	engage in trade	管理 guǎn lǐ	manage
茫茫 máng máng	boundless; vast	家務 jiā wù	housework
做買賣 zuò mǎi mai	do business	首飾 shǒu shi	jewelry
老闆 lǎo bǎn	boss	化妝品 huà zhuāng pǐn	cosmetics
招呼 zhāo hu	call	談 tán	talk
身材 shēn cái	stature; figure	封 fēng	confer upon
扭捏 niǔ nie	affectedly bashful	替 tì	for; substitute for
擦 cā	wipe	纏 chán	wrap; bind
胭脂 yān zhi	rouge (make up)	扶 fú	help; support
稀奇古怪 xī qí gǔ guài	peculiar; bizarre	得 děi	must; have to
彆扭 biè niu	uncomfortable; awkward	哀求 āi qiú	implore; plead

聽寫

經商　茫茫　招呼　擦　彆扭　化妝品　扶　家務

談　封　替　*纏　稀奇古怪

比一比

經 { 經商 / 經常 / 經過 }　　招 { 招呼 / 招待 / 招手 }　　扭 { 扭捏 / 彆扭 / 扭傷 }

首 { 首飾 / 首都 }　　化 { 化妝 / 化學 }　　談 { 談話 / 談價錢 }

詞語運用

經商
爸爸經商，所以常常出差。

彆扭
這件衣服穿起來很彆扭，一點兒也不舒(shū)服。

小妹妹太嬌氣，常常和小朋友鬧彆扭。

封

這是一封信，外面是信封，裏面是信紙。

女國王封林之洋做"娘娘"。

家務

我十二歲了，常常幫助媽媽做家務。

男孩子也應該做些家務。

反義詞

高大——矮小　　　　　　扭捏——大方

多音字

zhā
扎

zhā
扎 耳朵眼兒

zhá
扎

zhá
掙扎

回答問題

1. 林之洋願意做娘娘嗎？為什麼？
2. 什麼是美？請說一說你的看法。
3. 如果你是一個男孩兒，讀了《女兒國》以後有什麼想法？
4. 如果你是一個女孩兒，讀了《女兒國》以後有什麼想法？

詞語解釋

海外——國外。

不由分說——不管你願意不願意，不許你說明自己的意見。

稀奇古怪——新奇，很少見，與眾不同。

Lesson Two

The Kingdom of Women

  There once lived a scholar named Tang Ao in the Tang Dynasty who ventured overseas to do business with his two friends, Lin Zhiyang and Duo Jiugong.

  They had been sailing on the open sea for a long period when they finally spotted land one day. When they went ashore, they found that all the farmers, workers, and merchants they saw were women. These women not only talked loudly, they also dressed like men. Tang Ao and his friends were puzzled. They came to an inn and were welcomed by a woman in a man's attire. Introducing herself as the innkeeper, she turned and called for her servants. At her calling, a man in a woman's dress came out. Although he was a tall man with a beard, he walked and talked like a woman, and even had powder and rouge on his face. Tang Ao and his friends felt both strange and uncomfortable.

  Soon, Tang Ao and his friends realized that this was the Kingdom of Women, where women ruled and worked while men stayed home to do housework. Tang Ao and his friends spent the next few days doing business on the streets. One day, someone came to them, saying, "Your jewelry and cosmetics are excellent. Our king wants to purchase some for the palace 'maids' and invites you to the palace for business negotiations."

  Upon reaching the royal palace, something unexpected happened. The female ruler fell in love with Lin Zhiyang when she first laid eyes on him and promptly conferred upon him the title of an imperial concubine. Immediately, a large group of palace "maids" came forward. They changed Lin's clothes, put accessories and applied rouge on him. One maid saw that Lin had not pierced his ears and proceeded to pierce both his earlobes with needles, causing Lin to cry out in pain. Another saw that Lin's feet had not been bound. He took long strips of cloth and bound both of Lin's feet tightly. Lin could hardly walk without the help of others. He could not bear the pain and removed the cloth strips himself. The ruler found out about this and became very angry with Lin. She scolded him, saying, "How can you misbehave yourself in this manner? I must teach you a lesson." She then ordered for Lin to be beaten. Ignoring Lin's pleas, she commanded that Lin be locked up and that the wedding was to be held several days later.

Tang Ao and Duo Jiugong returned to the inn and contemplated for a long time before coming up with an idea. They remembered that according to Chinese customs, the bride must not live in her husband's house before the wedding. They said to the ruler, "Lin must return to the inn. Please send your men to escort him back to the palace on the wedding day." The ruler granted their request and let Lin go. But she also sent many guards to keep watch at the inn.

That night, under the cloak of darkness, Tang Ao and Duo Jiugong carried the injured Lin and sneaked out of the inn. They hurriedly boarded a boat and fled this strange Kingdom of Women.

(Excerpted and Abbreviated from *Flowers in the Mirror*)

第三課

草船借箭

諸葛亮是個才智過人的軍師，周瑜(yú)一直對他不服氣，總是刁難他。

這天，周瑜派人把諸葛亮請來，裝作請教的樣子，問他："先生，再過幾天，我們就要和曹軍打仗了，水陸交戰，用什麼兵器最好呢？"諸葛亮說："當然是弓箭好了。"周瑜一聽，連忙說："先生和我想的一樣。不過我軍缺少弓箭，想請先生負責趕造十萬支箭。打曹操是我們孫、劉兩家的事，希望先生不要推辭。"諸葛亮說："好說，好說。都督派我做這件事，我一定盡力。只是不知道您什麼時候要用這些箭？"周瑜說："你看十天完成，怎麼樣？"諸葛亮說："曹操大軍很快要進攻我們，如果花費十天時間造箭，恐怕會誤事。"

周瑜急忙又問："那你說幾天能完成呢？"

諸葛亮伸出三個手指，對周瑜說："三天之後，十萬支箭送給都督。"

三天造出十萬支箭，這是根本不可能的。周瑜一聽，立刻板起臉說："先生和我開玩笑嗎？"諸葛亮說："軍中無戲言，我

願意和都督簽下生死文書。如果三天造不出十萬支箭，你可以砍我的頭。"

周瑜一聽，心中大喜，當時就和諸葛亮立下了生死文書。諸葛亮說："今天來不及了，明天開始造。三天以後，請都督派五百士兵到江邊取箭。"

諸葛亮離開後，周瑜手下的人都奇怪地問："三天怎麼能造出十萬支箭？諸葛亮是不是在騙我們？"周瑜說："是他自己送死，不是我逼他的。如果到時候造不出來，想拖延時間，我就定他死罪。"

當天，周瑜派手下魯肅去諸葛亮那裏探聽情況。魯肅是諸葛亮的好朋友，他很替諸葛亮擔心。

諸葛亮見魯肅來了，就說："周瑜明明是要刁難我。十萬支箭，三天哪兒能造好？您一定要救我呀。"魯肅說："是你自己說大話，我怎麼救你？"諸葛亮說："請您幫我一個忙：借給我二十條船，每條船上有三十個士兵。這些船全部用黑布蒙好，還要有一千個稻草人擺放在船艙的兩邊，我自有妙用。這些秘密請您千萬不要對周都督說起。"

魯肅答應了。他不知道諸葛亮借船有什麼用。回去見到周瑜，他果然沒提借船的事。魯肅私自派了二十條快船，按照諸葛亮說的，用黑布把船遮好，船上擺上稻草人，等候諸葛亮調用。

第一天，不見諸葛亮的動靜；第二天，還不見諸葛亮的動靜；

直到第三天的深夜，諸葛亮突然跑來找魯肅，對魯肅說："我請您和我一起去取箭。"說著，拉著魯肅就上了船。

魯肅問："到哪裏取？"諸葛亮說："不用問，去了就知道了。"

諸葛亮吩咐用繩子把二十條船一個跟著一個連接起來，悄悄地朝江北岸划去。這時候，江上起了大霧，幾丈之外就看不見人影了。大約五點鐘時，船隊已經靠近曹軍水寨。諸葛亮命令士兵把船一字排開，又叫船上的士兵一邊敲鼓一邊大聲喊叫。他和魯肅卻坐在船艙中喝酒。

魯肅吃驚地問："咱們人這麼少，如果曹軍衝過來，怎麼辦？"諸葛亮笑著說："這樣大的霧，曹軍又不熟悉水戰，他們怎麼敢派兵出來？你就放心繼續喝酒吧。"

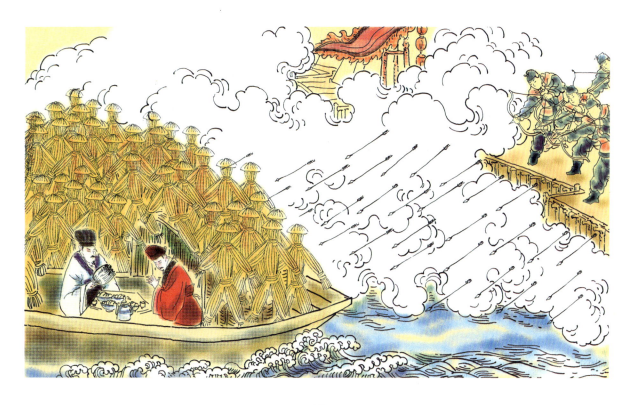

曹操聽到鼓聲和喊聲，以為敵人進攻了。他剛要下令出兵，又一想，江上這麼大的霧，敵人一定有埋伏，不該出去迎戰。於是傳令說："江上霧太大，不要輕易出動。多派弓箭手向敵人射箭，不要讓他們靠近。"

曹操派了一萬多個弓箭手來到江邊。他們一齊放箭。幾十萬支箭連續飛出，好像下雨一樣射到船上。只過了一會兒，船一側的稻草人身上就插滿了箭。諸葛亮又下令調轉船頭，讓船的另一側對著曹軍，仍舊讓士兵敲鼓喊叫。很快，船另一側的稻草人上也插滿了曹軍射來的箭。

太陽出來了，江面上的霧慢慢散去。只見二十條船兩側的稻草人身上全都插滿了箭。諸葛亮一看，大功告成，就下令快速開船返回，又讓士兵齊聲大喊："謝曹丞相[chéng]①送箭！"等到曹操明白上當了，諸葛亮的船早已開出二十多里，追也來不及了。

二十條船靠岸的時候，周瑜派來的五百士兵正好前來取箭。每條船上大約有五六千支箭，二十條船總共有十萬多支。

魯肅把諸葛亮借箭的經過告訴了周瑜，周瑜長嘆一聲，說："諸葛亮神機妙算，我真不如他。"

（根據羅貫中著《三國演義》選段改編）

---

① 丞相——古代王朝職[zhí]位最高的大臣。

作品簡介

　　《三國演義》是中國古代優秀的長篇歷史小說。作者羅貫中是元末明初人（約1330—1400）。《三國演義》描寫了東漢末年和三國時期曹操、劉備、孫權三者之間在軍事、政治、外交等幾個方面的鬥爭。作者筆下的戰爭充滿了鬥智鬥勇的精彩情節，其中"草船借箭"、"借東風"等故事生動、神奇，廣為流傳。諸葛亮是全書的中心人物，他具有傑出的智慧和非凡的軍事指揮才能，在中國人的心目中已成為智慧的化身。

本文人物

諸葛亮：西蜀劉備的軍師。　　周瑜：東吳孫權的都督。
魯肅：東吳的大臣，諸葛亮的朋友。　　曹操：漢朝丞相。

生詞

zhū gě 諸葛	Zhuge (surname)	kǒng pà 恐怕	be afraid
cái zhì 才智	ability and wisdom	wù shì 誤事	mess things
diāo nàn 刁難	make things difficult	qiān zì 簽（字）	sign
fù zé 負責	responsible	tuō yán 拖延	delay
tuī cí 推辭	decline	lǔ 魯	Lu (surname)
dū du 都督	military commander	shuō dà huà 說大話	brag; boast
jìn gōng 進攻	attack	mì mì 秘密	secret
huā fèi 花費	spend	sī zì 私自	privately; secretly

zhē 遮	cover	dí rén 敵人	enemy
bǎi 擺	put; place	mái fú 埋伏	ambush
fēn fù 吩咐	instruct	réng jiù 仍舊	still; remain the same
shuǐzhài 水寨	military fort in water	sàn qù 散去	disperse
qiāo gǔ 敲鼓	beat on the drums	shén jī miàosuàn 神機妙算	amazing foresight

聽寫

敵人　恐怕　拖延　仍舊　散去　吩咐　私自　秘密

神機妙算　擺　花費　*進攻　遮

比一比

{ 逼（逼著）
　幅（一幅畫）
　福（幸福）

{ 刁（刁難）
　叼（叼著肉）

{ 仍（仍舊）
　扔（扔下）

詞語運用

秘密

我有個小秘密：母親節要送給媽媽一張我畫的賀卡。

恐怕

電影要開始了，我們現在不走，恐怕就來不及了。

你現在纔去機場，恐怕趕不上飛機了。

推辭

晚會上同學們請小龍表演功夫，他沒有推辭，馬上就表演了。

反義詞

敵人——朋友　　　　　推辭——接受

多音字

相 xiāng
相 xiāng { 相信 / 互相 }

相 xiàng
相 xiàng { 照相 / 丞相 }

難 nàn
難 nàn { 刁難 / 難民 }

難 nán
難 nán { 難受 / 艱難 }

méng　　　　　　　　　měng
蒙　　　　　　　　　　蒙
méng　　　　　　　　　měng
蒙上　　　　　　　　　蒙古

回答問題

1. 周瑜讓諸葛亮負責造箭，他的目(dì)的是什麼？

2. 諸葛亮為什麼向魯肅借船，又不讓他告訴周瑜？

3. 請試著講一講諸葛亮是如何用草船向曹軍借箭的。

4. 選做題：想一想，為什麼直到第三天諸葛亮纔去取箭？

詞語解釋

板起臉——不高興，臉上沒有笑容。

軍中無戲言——軍隊中討論作戰時，不可以開玩笑。

生死文書——一種完不成任務自願受死的保證書。

大功告成——指大的工程、重要的任務宣告完成。

輕易——簡單、容易；隨隨便便。

Lesson Three

Using Straw Boats to Borrow Arrows

Zhuge Liang was a military strategist with outstanding talent. However, Zhou Yu did not think likewise and often tried to make things difficult for him.

One day, Zhou Yu sent for Zhuge Liang. Pretending to be seeking his advice, he asked, "Mr. Zhuge, we will be going into battle in a few days with Cao Cao's army on both land and sea. What would be the best weapon for us?" Zhuge Liang answered, "Bows and arrows, of course." At this, Zhou Yu immediately said, "I think so too. But our army lacks arrows. Would you please be in charge of producing 100,000 arrows for our army? This is important so please don't decline." Zhuge Liang replied, "You are the military commander. I will definitely try my best to accomplish this task. When would you need the arrows?" Zhou Yu said, "How about 10 days?" Zhuge Liang shook his head and replied, "The army of Cao Cao will be attacking us soon. I'm afraid 10 days would be too long a time."

Zhou Yu quickly responded, "How many days do you think you'll need?"

Showing three fingers, Zhuge Liang said to Zhou Yu, "Three days. I'll give you 100,000 arrows within three days."

To produce 100,000 arrows in three days was an impossible feat, and Zhou Yu knew it. He asked, "Are you joking with me?" Zhuge Liang said, "There's no joking about military matters. I'm willing to sign a contract with you. If I'm unable to give you 100,000 arrows in three days, you may execute me."

Zhou Yu was pleased and signed the covenant with Zhuge Liang immediately. Then Zhuge Liang said, "It's too late to begin today. I'll start tomorrow. Three days later, please send 500 soldiers to the riverside to collect the arrows."

After Zhuge Liang had left, Zhou Yu's men asked, "How can 100,000 arrows be produced in three days? Is Zhuge Liang playing any tricks on us?" Zhou Yu said, "This is his own suggestion; I didn't force him into it. If he fails to deliver and asks for more time, I will sentence him to death immediately."

Later that day, Zhou Yu sent one of his men, Lu Su, to visit Zhuge Liang to find out what was happening. Lu Su was a good friend of Zhuge Liang, and he was worried for his friend.

Zhuge Liang said to Lu Su, "It is obvious that Zhou Yu wants to make things difficult for me. How would it be possible to produce 100,000 arrows in three days? You've got to help me." Lu Su replied, "It was you who boasted that it's possible. How can I help you now?" Zhuge Liang answered, "Please do me a favor. Lend me 20 boats with 30 soldiers in each boat. Cover these boats with black cloth and place 1,000 scarecrows along both sides of each boat. This is confidential, don't mention it to Commander Zhou."

Lu Su agreed to help but had no idea why Zhuge Liang would want so many boats. He returned to see Zhou Yu but did not mention anything about the boats. Lu Su privately set aside 20 fast boats with scarecrows and covered them with black cloth as instructed by Zhuge Liang.

On the first day, Zhuge Liang did nothing. On the second day, Zhuge Liang did nothing either. It was only on the third night when Zhuge Liang went looking for Lu Su. He said, "I invite you to fetch those arrows with me." With that, he boarded the boat with Lu Su.

Lu Su asked, "Where are we going?" Zhuge Liang replied, " Don't ask, you'll know when you get there."

Zhuge Liang instructed that the 20 boats be connected together with ropes and they quietly set sail toward the north bank of the river. At that time, there was a dense fog over the river, making it impossible to see clearly. Before dawn, the boats neared the fort where Cao's army was stationed. Zhuge Liang ordered the soldiers to arrange all the boats in a single line. Then he got them to beat war drums and shout battle cries. In the meantime, he sat inside the boat with Lu Su, drinking.

Astounded, Lu Su asked, "We have so few men. What shall we do if Cao's army attacks?" Zhuge Liang laughed and said, "With such a dense fog, Cao Cao would not dare to send his army out. He's not familiar with battle in water. Relax and drink."

Cao Cao heard the war drums and battle cries. Thinking that the enemy was beginning to launch their attack, he was about to dispatch his troops to fight but he thought about it again, "The enemy must have laid an ambush in such a dense fog. We mustn't sail out." So he ordered his soldiers to stay and said, "The fog is too dense and we don't know the exact situation out there. Let's not make any hasty moves. Send archers to shoot at them and don't let them come any closer."

Cao Cao sent more than 10,000 archers to the riverbank and they shot arrows at the boats. The arrows fell like rain on the boats and soon the scarecrows on one side of the boats were filled with arrows. Zhuge Liang ordered that all the boats be turned around such that the other side of the boats will face Cao Cao's army and told the soldiers to drum and shout as before. In no time, the scarecrows on the other side of the boats were also filled with arrows.

When the sun rose, the fog began to clear. Seeing that the scarecrows along both sides of the boats were filled with arrows, Zhuge Liang knew his plan had succeeded and ordered for the boats to leave quickly. He also got the soliders to yell "Thank you Prime Minister Cao for giving us arrows!" When Cao Cao realized that he had been fooled, Zhuge Liang's boats had already sailed 20 miles away and could no longer be caught.

When the 20 boats approached the shore, they were met by the 500 soldiers sent by Zhou Yu to fetch the arrows. There were about five to six thousand arrows in one boat and a total of more than 100,000 arrows in all 20 boats.

Lu Su told Zhou Yu how Zhuge Liang had "borrowed" the arrows from Cao Cao. Zhou Yu sighed and said, "Zhuge Liang indeed has amazing foresight; I pale in comparison to him."

(Excerpted and Abbreviated from *Romance of the Three Kingdoms*)

第四課

孫悟空三打白骨精

這一天,唐僧師徒四人來到一座高山前面。唐僧說:"悟空,我肚子餓了,咱們找個地方休息一下,你去找些吃的東西來吧。"

悟空一個筋斗跳到雲端,四處一望,没有村莊人家,只見南山有一片桃林,於是對唐僧說:"這裏深山野谷,没有人家,我去南山摘些桃給您吃。"他又吩咐八戒、沙僧好好保護師父,就直奔南山而去。

不想這山裏有個妖精,她看見唐僧坐在地上,心中歡喜:

"運氣，運氣！早就聽說有個去西天取經的唐僧，如果誰能吃他一塊肉就能長生不老。今天他果然來了。"可是她看見八戒、沙僧守在唐僧身旁，一時無法下手。

妖精想了一個辦法，她搖身一變，變成一個年輕的女子，提著一個陶罐，朝唐僧走來。

唐僧見了，對八戒和沙僧說："悟空纔說這深山野谷，沒有人家，那不是個女子走過來了？"八戒見那女子長得美麗，連忙上前細聲問道："女菩薩，請問手裏提的是什麼東西？往哪裏去啊？"那妖精回答說："我這罐子裏是香米飯，到這裏來是給長老送飯的。"

八戒聽了，滿心歡喜。唐僧卻問道："女菩薩，你家住哪裏？你怎麼要給和尚送飯呢？"妖精編了一套假話，說："我家住在山下，丈夫在北山幹活，這飯是送給他的。不想遇到三位長老，這飯就敬長老吧。"

唐僧說："多謝了，多謝了！我有個徒弟摘桃子去了，一會兒就回來。我們要是吃了你的飯，你丈夫就沒有飯吃了。"這下可急壞了旁邊的豬八戒，他噘(juē)著嘴埋怨說："天下和尚多得很，可沒有一個像師父這樣不知好歹。現成的飯，三個人不吃，等那猴子回來，就得分成四份了。"不由分說，把罐子提過來就要吃。

正在這時，悟空拿著桃子回來了。他一眼就認出這個女子是個妖精，舉起棒子，當頭就打！唐僧嚇得忙上前攔住說："悟空，不要隨便傷人！"悟空說："師父，她是個妖精，是來騙你的，不要上當(dàng)。"

悟空照著妖精又是一棒。那妖精也有辦法：把一個假屍留在地面，自己卻化成一陣清風逃走了。

唐僧嚇得說："實在無禮！實在無禮！悟空，你竟敢無故傷人？"悟空說："師父不要怪罪，你看看這罐子裏裝的是什麼東西？"唐僧一看，哪裏是什麼香米飯？全是綠皮青蛙！這纔有幾分相信。可是八戒卻在旁邊挑撥說："這女子明明是個農婦，哥哥的棍子重，打死了她，怕你唸緊箍(gū zhòu)咒，故意用這個辦法騙我們。"唐僧聽了八戒的挑撥，信以為真，唸起了緊箍咒。悟空大叫："頭疼，頭疼！師父，別唸了，有話好說！"唐僧生氣地說："出家人連螞蟻都不傷害，怎能隨便傷人性命？像你這種人，就是取來真經，又有何用？我不要你這個徒弟了！"悟空見唐僧真的生了氣，連忙跪下叩(kòu)頭。唐僧說："這回饒了你。如果再作惡，我就唸二十遍緊箍咒。""三十遍也由你，只是我以後不打人了。"悟空說。

再說那妖精躲到雲裏，恨得咬牙切齒。她見唐僧、八戒沒認出她的真面目，心中暗暗高興。沒等唐僧走多遠，她搖身一變，變成一個老太太，拄著個棍子，一步一哭地走了過來。八戒見了，慌忙對唐僧說："師父，不好了，這老媽媽找女兒來了。"悟空一看那老婆婆，又是妖精變的，便把師父唸緊箍咒的事忘得一乾二淨，舉棒就打。那妖精慌忙一變，逃出真身，把老婆婆的假屍留在地上。

唐僧驚得落下馬來，他二話不說，一連唸了二十遍緊箍咒。悟空疼得連連在地上打滾。唐僧說悟空沒心行善，一會兒就打死兩個人。悟空爭辯說："她是妖精！她是妖精！"唐僧不由分說，又趕悟空走。悟空就求唐僧說："師父真不要我，就請把我頭上的箍給拿掉吧，我就快活了。"唐僧為難地說："菩薩沒教我鬆箍咒啊！"悟空道："既然沒有鬆箍咒，你還是帶我走吧。"

唐僧一行走了不遠，突然看見一個老頭兒，拄著棍子，一面走一面唸經。悟空一看那老頭兒，又是妖精變的，便拔根毫毛一吹，變成假悟空和妖精打，自己叫來山神、土地①說："這妖精三次害我師父，你們在空中四面把守，不許讓她逃了！"那妖精這次無處可逃，被孫悟空打死在地。

唐僧見悟空又把老頭兒打死，嚇得說不出話來。八戒在一旁冷笑道："好悟空，真發瘋了，半天就打死了三個人！"唐僧聽了，正要唸緊箍咒，悟空急忙來到馬前，大聲說："師父別唸，你快來看看妖精的模樣。"唐僧上前一看，很是驚奇。原來是一堆白骨，上面有四個字"白骨夫人"。唐僧也就相信悟空了。可八戒又挑撥說："師父，他打死了人，怕你唸咒，使個法子騙我們。"

---

① 山神、土地——傳說中管理一個地方的山和土地的神仙。

唐僧信了八戒的話，又唸緊箍咒。悟空疼得跪下說："師父，別唸了，別唸了！"唐僧說："這次我再也不能留你了，快走吧！"

悟空說："師父錯怪了我。那明明是個妖精，一心想害你。我把她打死，你卻聽那呆子的胡言亂語，好壞不分，一定趕我走！俗話說，'事不過三'。如果我再不走，也就太沒臉沒皮了。我走！我走！師父，今天我不得不離開。請你坐下，受我一拜。"唐僧把身子扭過去，說："我是一個好和尚，不受你惡人拜。"悟空拔出三根毫毛，吹了口仙氣，叫聲："變！"變出三個悟空，加上自己本身，共四個，四面圍著唐僧下拜，唐僧左右躲不開，只得受了一拜。

悟空拜完師父，對沙僧說："兄弟，你是個好人。要留心八戒的花言巧語，路上更要仔細。如果有妖精拿住師父，你就說老孫是他的大徒弟。那些妖怪知道我的手段，不敢傷害師父。"唐僧說："我們好和尚，不提你惡人的名字，你快離開這裏吧！"

悟空見唐僧怎麼也不肯回心轉意，只得含著眼淚告別了師父，一個筋斗回到了花果山，做起自由自在的美猴王來。

（根據吳承恩著《西遊記》選段改編）

作品簡介

《西遊記》是中國明代的一部長篇神話小說，作者是吳承恩（約1504—1582）。書中講述了唐僧和徒弟孫悟空、豬八戒、沙和尚去西天取經的故事。

　　孫悟空是《西遊記》中的主要人物。他是一位神話英雄，也是人們最喜愛的美猴王。他神通廣大，會七十二種變化；他機智勇敢，什麼都不怕，打敗了一路上碰到的所有妖精，保護唐僧到達西天，取到了真經。

　　《西遊記》是中國少年兒童最喜歡閱讀的書籍之一。

生詞

wù kōng 悟空	Wukong (*a name*)	jiǎ shī 假屍	fake corpse
táng sēng 唐僧	Tangseng (*a name* 僧: *monk*)	tiǎo bō 挑撥	incite
jīn dǒu 筋斗	somersault	è 惡	evil
bā jiè 八戒	Bajie (*a name*)	zhǔ zhe 拄著	lean on (a stick)
yāo jing 妖精	demon	zhēng biàn 爭辯	argue
yùn qi 運氣	fortune; luck	wéi nán 為難	feel embarrassed
pú sà 菩薩	Bodhisattva; Buddha	háo máo 毫毛	body hair
tú dì 徒弟	disciple; apprentice	fā fēng 發瘋	gone mad
hǎo dǎi 好歹	good and evil	mú yàng 模樣	appearance
bàng zi 棒子	stick	dāi zi 呆子	simpleton; foolish person
lán zhù 攔住	stop; hold back	liú xīn 留心	pay attention to
suí biàn 隨便	as one pleases	qiǎo 巧	cunning; skillful

32

聽寫

攔住　惡　模樣　好歹　發瘋　拄著　花言巧語

隨便　呆　棒子　挑撥　*毫毛　爭辯

比一比

模（模樣）
摸（摸一摸）
漠（沙漠）

拄（拄著）
柱（柱子）

屍（假屍）
屋（屋子）

撥（挑撥）
潑（活潑）

吩（吩咐）
分（分開）

咐（吩咐）
附（附近）

詞語運用

隨便
大家別客氣，想吃什麼隨便挑。
上課不要隨便說話，有問題請舉手。

埋怨
同學們全都埋怨這次考試太難了。
弟弟寫不好字，不是埋怨筆不好，就是埋怨紙不好。

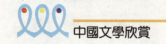

爭辯

妹妹爭辯說："玩具不是我弄壞的。"

悟空爭辯說："師父，她是妖精！"

反義詞

好——歹　　善——惡　　舉起——放下

笨——巧　　鬆——緊

多音字

mú	mó
模	模
mú	mó
模樣	模特（兒）

děi	dé
得	得
děi	dé
就得	得到

tiǎo	tiāo
挑	挑
tiǎo	tiāo
挑撥	挑水

回答問題

1. 你喜歡孫悟空嗎？為什麼？

2. 唐僧為什麼容易相信八戒的話而不愛聽悟空的話？

3. 唐僧是個明白人還是個糊塗人？

4. 你要是悟空的話，離開唐僧以後還回來嗎？

5. 唐僧取經是不是需要"團隊精神"？

詞語解釋

咬牙切齒——咬緊牙，表示痛恨。

不知好歹——不知道好壞。

回心轉意——改變主意，又回到原來的想法。

花言巧語——用好聽的話騙人。

自由自在——能夠按自己的願望活動，不受別人管。

手段——辦法。

上當——受騙吃虧。

無故——沒有原因。

Lesson Four

The Monkey King Defeats the White Bone Demon Three Times

One day, Master Tangseng and his three disciples arrived at the foot of a high mountain. Tangseng said to his eldest disciple, "Wukong, I'm hungry. Let's find a place to rest and you can try to get some food for us."

Wukong somersaulted onto a cloud and looked around, but did not see any villages. He spotted a peach forest near a mountain in the south and said to the master, "There are no houses nearby. I'll go to the south to get some peaches for you." He then instructed Bajie and Shaseng to protect their master and hurried toward the south.

Now, there was a bone demon in the mountain. When she saw Tangseng sitting on the ground at the foot of the mountain, she was delighted. "Lucky me! I've heard that Tangseng is going to the West to retrieve the Buddhist scriptures and should anyone eat a piece of his flesh, they can live forever. And here he is today!" she thought. But she saw that Bajie and Shaseng were guarding their master and could not find a way to attack Tangseng.

Then she had an idea. Transforming herself into a young lady, she carried a clay jar and approached Tangseng.

The master saw her and said to his two disciples, "Just now Wukong said that there were no houses nearby, but isn't that a lady coming our way?" The lady was so pretty that Bajie quickly greeted her, saying gently, "Young lady, what do you have in your arms, and where are you going?" The demon replied, "I have fragrant rice in the jar and have come to offer it to you."

At this, Bajie was pleased. But Tangseng asked, "Please, may I ask where your home is and why have you come to give alms to monks?" The demon lied to him, saying, "I live at the foot of the mountain and my husband works in the northern mountain. The rice was meant for him. But since I've met you, you may have it."

Tangseng declined her offer politely, saying, "Thank you, thank you very much! But one of my disciples has gone to pick peaches for us and will be back soon. If we have your rice, your husband would have nothing to eat." Bajie was impatient at hearing this and complained, "There're so many monks in the world but none is like my master who doesn't know any better. There are only three of us now, and when that monkey returns, we'll have to divide the rice into four portions." Not wanting to wait any longer, he took the jar, and was about to eat the rice.

At that moment, Wukong returned with the peaches. He saw through the demon's disguise at once and he raised his stick and hit the demon. Tangseng immediately stopped him, saying, "Wukong, you must not hurt people as you please." Wukong replied, "But master, she is a demon and is trying to fooling you. Don't believe her words."

第四課

Wukong continued hitting the demon. However, the demon was cunning and she left a false corpse on the ground while she transformed herself into a draught of wind and escaped.

Tangseng exclaimed, "How could you be so barbaric? How dare you kill innocent people at will!" Wukong explained, "Master, don't blame me. Look what's inside the jar." Tangseng looked into the jar and saw that instead of fragrant rice, it was filled with green frogs. He began to believe Wukong, but Bajie said, "That lady is clearly a peasant woman. Elder brother has killed her with his stick. But he is fooling us with these frogs because he's afraid of your chant that tightens the magical headband around his head." Upon hearing Bajie's words, Tangseng believed him and began to recite the incantation that causes the band on Wukong's head to tighten. Wukong cried out in pain and begged his master to stop, "My head! My head! Please, master, stop chanting. We can talk this over." Tangseng said angrily, "A monk would not even kill an ant. How can you kill people as you please? Even if we have the Buddhist scriptures now, what's the point with people like you? I don't want you to be my disciple!" Realizing that the master was really angry, Wukong quickly knelt down and kowtowed to him. Tangseng said, "I shall forgive you this time. If you do evil again, I shall chant the incantation 20 times." Wukong replied, "You can say it 30 times but I won't hit people again."

Hiding in a cloud, the demon clenched her teeth in hatred. But she was glad that both Tangseng and Bajie could not detect her true self. After Tangseng and his disciples had walked for a while more, she transformed herself into an old lady with a walking stick, crying while walking toward them. Bajie panicked and said to Tangseng, "Oh no! This old lady must be looking for her daughter." Wukong, however, saw that the old lady was really the demon in disguise and forgot all about the earlier episode with his master. Raising his stick, he hit the demon. The demon escaped once again, leaving behind a false corpse of the old lady on the ground.

Tangseng was so astounded by Wukong's actions that he dismounted his horse. Without hesitation, he repeated the chant 20 times, causing Wukong to roll on the ground in excruciating pain. Tangseng scolded Wukong for not having the heart to do good and for killing two innocent persons within such a short span of time. Wukong defended himself and argued, "She is a demon. A demon, master!" Tangseng refused to listen to his explanations and once again demanded that he leave. Wukong pleaded, "If you don't want me to follow you any longer, please remove the band on my head and I'll be contented." "But Guanyin did not teach me the chant for loosening the band," said Tangseng. Wukong replied, "Since you don't know how to loosen my band, then you have to take me along with you."

Tangseng and his disciples continued on their journey. Suddenly, they saw an old man with a walking stick, chanting scriptures while approaching them. Wukong saw that it was the same demon in disguise. He pulled out a strand of his hair and blew on it. It transformed into a clone of himself and fought with the demon. In the meantime, Wukong's true self summoned the local mountain and earth gods. He said to them, "This demon has tried to harm my master three times. Guard the four directions in the air and don't let her escape again." This time, the demon could not escape and was finally killed by Wukong.

Tangseng became speechless when he saw that Wukong had killed the old man. Bajie sneered and said, "What a brave Wukong! Are you mad? You've killed three persons in half a day!" At Bajie's

words, Tangseng was about to say the chant again when Wukong hurried to him and explained, "Master, please don't say the chant. Come see for yourself what the demon is really like." Tangseng went forward and was shocked to find a pile of bones. Inscribed on top were the words "Lady White Bone". Tangseng was about to believe Wukong when Bajie incited him once more, saying, "Master, he's just afraid that you'll say the chant because he killed people. He's fooling us."

Tangseng listened Bajie's words and began to chant again. The pain was so great that Wukong knelt down, saying, "Please, master, stop chanting." Tangseng said, "I won't keep you this time. Leave now!"

Wukong said, "Master, you've wronged me. That was a demon who wanted to harm you. I killed her to save you and yet you believe Bajie's nonsense. Without discerning good from evil, you insist that I leave. There's a saying, 'Wrong things should not happen more than three times.' If I don't leave, then shame on me. I'll go! I'll go! Master, I'm leaving now. Please sit down and allow me to kowtow to you one last time." Tangseng turned away and said, "I'm a good monk. I won't accept a kowtow from an evil person like you." Wukong pulled out three strands of hair, blew on them and transformed them into three clones of himself. The four of them surrounded Tangseng and kowtowed to him. Unable to turn away, Tangseng had no choice but to accept this last bow from Wukong.

Wukong then said to Shaseng, "You are a good man. Be careful of Bajie's sweet words and keep a lookout during the journey. If master is caught by any demon, just tell them that I'm his eldest disciple. The demons know me and would not dare to harm master." Tangseng replied, "We're good monks and won't mention the name of an evil person like you. Leave now!"

Seeing that Tangseng would not change his mind, Wukong bid his master farewell with tears in his eyes. He jumped high into the air and returned home to Huaguoshan where he became a Monkey King again.

(Excerpted and Abbreviated from *Journey to the West*)

第五課

雞毛信

故事發生在抗日戰爭時期。那一年海娃十四歲,是龍門村兒童團①的團長。

一天傍晚,海娃正在山上一邊放羊,一邊放哨。這時候,從小路上急急忙忙地走來一個人,老遠就叫:"海娃!海娃!"海娃聽出是爸爸的聲音,連忙迎上去。爸爸從懷裏拿出一封信,對海娃說:"馬上到王莊去,把信送給民兵隊張隊長。"海娃接過信一看,信上插著三根雞毛,他知道這是一封很緊急的信。海娃收好信,趕著羊群就走了。

---

① 兒童團——抗日戰爭時期,由兒童組成的團體。

誰知走到山腳下，海娃忽然看見西山頂上的"消息樹"①倒了。糟糕！一定是有日本兵。海娃回頭一看，果然來了一隊搶糧的日本兵。

日本兵越走越近。海娃著急了，把雞毛信藏在哪裏呢？他看著胖乎乎的羊尾巴，心頭一動，趕快抱住那隻帶頭的老綿羊，把雞毛信綁在了它的尾巴底下。海娃站起來，把放羊的鞭子甩得"啪(pā)啪"響，趕著羊群朝日本兵走過去。

"站住！"日本兵喊起來，"嘩(huā)啦"一聲，舉起槍，對著海娃的腦袋。一個穿黑軍裝的歪嘴黑狗②跑過來，一把抓住海娃，把他拉到一個長著小鬍子的日本兵面前。海娃一點兒也不怕，他故意歪著腦袋，張著大嘴，傻乎乎地望著小鬍子。小鬍子說聲："搜！"那個歪嘴黑狗馬上動手，把海娃周身都搜了一遍，連兩隻穿破的鞋也沒放過，可是什麼也沒搜出來。小鬍子只想早點進山去搶糧食，就衝著海娃喊："滾開！滾開！"海娃回頭就跑。沒想到，那個歪嘴黑狗又追上來，用槍逼著海娃，要海娃趕著羊跟他們走。他說："我們還沒吃飯呢！這麼些羊，夠我們吃的啦！"海娃沒有辦法，只好跟著走。

太陽落山了，日本兵的隊伍停在一個小村莊裏，宰了幾隻

---

① 消息樹——抗日戰爭時期，華北農村地區專門傳送危急消息的樹。樹立著，表示平安無事；樹倒下，表示敵人來了。

② 黑狗——抗日戰爭時期，老百姓對穿黑軍裝的中國偽(wěi)權(quán)軍人的稱呼。

羊，燒羊肉吃。海娃顧不上心疼他的羊了，悄悄地把手伸到老綿羊的大尾巴下面一摸，雞毛信還在呢！他放心了。日本兵吃飽了，一個個摸著肚皮，睡覺去了。歪嘴黑狗叫海娃把羊趕進圈裏，又把海娃拉進屋裏。日本兵和黑狗們抱著槍睡在乾草上，把海娃放在最裏頭。

海娃睡不著，他想："日本兵明天還要宰羊，要是今晚跑不掉，雞毛信可就完了。"這時遠處傳來雞叫聲，海娃再也躺不住了。他坐起來一看，門口的哨兵睡著了。他就悄悄地站起來，閃到門邊，又輕輕地邁過哨兵的大腿，溜到了羊圈，抱住那隻老綿羊，把它尾巴下面的雞毛信解下來，放進口袋裏，一口氣跑上了山。

天亮了，海娃爬上了山頂，聽見前面有人叫喚。他抬頭一看，山那頭有個日本兵拿著面小白旗，朝著海娃來回搖晃。海娃脫下身上的白布上衣，學著日本兵的樣子也來回搖晃。沒想到，真混過去了。海娃跑下山，一口氣跑到了對面山頂。前面就是王莊啦，海娃高興極了。他一屁股坐在山頭上，把手伸進口袋一摸，不覺渾身哆嗦起來。雞毛信呢？口袋裏沒有啦。海娃趕緊脫下上衣來找，也沒有；把身邊的石頭縫都找遍了，還是沒有。海娃馬上往回跑，沿著來的路一邊跑一邊找。他又一口氣爬上山，山頂上，就在剛才搖晃衣服的地方，雞毛信好好地躺在那兒。海娃高興極了，把信裝進口袋，剛想往回跑，忽然聽見背後有人喊叫，歪嘴黑狗追上來了。他抓住海娃，叫海娃回去給日本兵帶路。

小鬍子把洋刀一揮，日本兵和黑狗又出發了。海娃趕著羊群夾在他們中間，來到了一個山溝，王莊就在前面那座山上。海娃看到山上的"消息樹"放倒了，不用説，張隊長的隊伍已經知道日本兵來了。日本兵可什麼也不知道，他們在山溝裏坐下休息，又是喝水，又是抽煙。

休息夠了，一隊黑狗先走，上了山。山坡上忽然"轟轟"幾聲巨響，冒起一柱一柱的黑煙，黑狗踩上地雷了。小鬍子指著山路對海娃説："你在前面帶路，我們跟在後面。明白嗎？"海娃遠遠地走在日本兵的前邊。山坡上有一片樹林。樹林裏出現了一個岔路口：一條小路，一條羊道。海娃把羊趕上了羊道。歪嘴黑狗在後面叫道："走錯了！"海娃大聲説："沒錯！我走過的。放心走吧！"羊道越來越不好走。日本兵走走停停，遠遠地落在了後面。小鬍子心生懷疑，吼叫起來："慢慢的！"海娃裝作沒聽見，一步緊一步地往前跑。日本兵使勁喊："站住！再不站住就開槍啦！"海娃不理他，甩了一響鞭，拼命往前跑。日本兵真的開槍了。海娃跑著跑著，實在跑不動了，一頭就撲倒在亂草裏，大聲叫："日本兵上來啦！打呀！趕快打呀！"山頂上突然響起一陣槍聲。海娃聽出來了，這是自己人的槍聲……

等海娃睜開眼睛，看見在他身邊的正是張隊長。張隊長關心地問他:"還疼嗎?"海娃顧不得回答,連忙說:"信……雞毛信……"張隊長哈哈大笑起來。他摸著海娃的腦袋,說:"放心吧,信已經收到了。你把日本兵帶到沒有路的地方,咱們的隊伍就把日本兵消滅了。謝謝你這個小英雄!"

(根據華山著《雞毛信》改編)

生詞

cūn zhuāng 村莊	village	chī bǎo 吃飽	eat one's fill
ér tóng 兒童	children	liū 溜	sneak off
fàng shào 放哨	be on patrol	jiào huan 叫喚	call; cry
jǐn jí 緊急	urgent	tuō 脫	take off
qiǎng 搶	rob; snatch	duō suo 哆嗦	tremble; shiver
miányáng 綿羊	sheep	fèng 縫	crevice
bǎng 綁	bind; tie	huī 揮	wield
biān zi 鞭子	whip; lash	chōuyān 抽煙	smoke
sōu 搜	search	chà lù 岔路	fork in the road; crossroad
gù bu shàng 顧不上	regardless of	pīn mìng 拼命	exert one's utmost strength

中國文學欣賞

聽寫

村莊　兒童　搶　吃飽　溜　脫　顧不上　緊急　拼命　揮　叫喚　放哨

比一比

- 村（村莊）
- 寸（尺寸）

- 童（兒童）
- 撞（撞倒）

- 喚（叫喚）
- 換（調換）

- 傍（傍晚）
- 旁（旁邊）

- 搶（搶糧）
- 槍（手槍）

- 飽（吃飽）
- 包（書包）

- 拼（拼命）
- 併（合併）

- 溜（溜走）
- 留（留下）

- 哨（放哨）
- 消（消息）

詞語運用

溜

大華今天上課遲到了，他輕輕打開教室的門溜了進去。

每年冬天她都去溜冰。

會還沒有開完，他就悄悄地溜走了。

拼命

小兔子拼命地跑進了樹林，老鷹沒有抓著它。

他幹活真拼命，比誰幹得都多。

找出近義詞

喊叫　　妖精　　附近　　小孩

叫喚（　　）　兒童（　　）　旁邊（　　）　鬼（　　）

反義詞

傍晚──早晨　　　　　飽──餓　　　擔心──放心

綁上──解開　　　　　脫──穿　　　歪──正

多音字

chòng
衝

chōng
衝

chòng
衝著

chōng
衝突

juàn
圈

quān
圈

juàn
羊圈

quān
圓圈

落 luò
luò
落葉

落 là
là
丟三落四

回答問題

1. 故事發生在什麼時候？

2. 信上有三根雞毛是什麼意思？

3. 海娃遇見鬼子時把雞毛信藏在哪裏了？

4. 雞毛信丟過沒有？怎麼找回來的？

5. 海娃把鬼子帶到哪裏了？

6. 張隊長收到雞毛信了嗎？

詞語解釋

趕緊——趕快，連忙。

心疼——捨不得，珍惜。

顧不上——照管不了。

消滅——消失，滅亡。

Lesson Five

The Letter with Feathers

This story is placed during the Anti-Japanese War period and it is about a fourteen-year-old Haiwa who was the scout leader in Longmen Village.

One evening, Haiwa was on patrol herding sheep. A man called out urgently to him from a small path nearby, "Haiwa! Haiwa!" Haiwa recognized his father's voice and ran toward him. His father took out a letter and said to him, "Go to the Wang Village immediately and pass this letter to Militia Commander Zhang." Haiwa took the letter and saw three feathers attached to it. He understood that the message was urgent. Keeping the letter carefully, Haiwa left with the herd of sheep.

When he reached the foot of the mountain, Haiwa noticed that the tree on the top of the western mountain had fallen and this was a signal to mean that the Japanese army had arrived. Haiwa turned and saw a troop of Japanese soldiers approaching.

As the Japanese soldiers drew near, Haiwa began to get anxious. Where should he hide the letter? Seeing the sheep's fat tail, Haiwa had an idea. He quickly caught hold of the old sheep that was leading the herd and tied the letter tightly beneath its tail. Then Haiwa stood up, wielded the whip, and drove the sheep toward the Japanese soldiers.

"Freeze!" shouted the Japanese soldiers, pointing their guns at Haiwa's head. A Chinese puppet soldier (a Chinese traitor) in black uniform ran over, caught hold of Haiwa, and brought him to a Japanese soldier with a moustache. Haiwa was not afraid at all. He deliberately cocked his head, opened his mouth wide, and looked at the soldier in a silly manner. The soldier with the moustache ordered, "Search him." The Chinese puppet soldier obeyed immediately and searched all parts of Haiwa's body, including his two worn-out shoes. But he found nothing. With his mind focused on going into the mountain to snatch food grains as soon as possible, the moustached soldier shouted at Haiwa, "Get out of here! Get out!" Haiwa turned and ran away immediately. To his surprise, the Chinese puppet soldier caught up with him and threatened Haiwa with a gun. The soldier ordered him to follow them with his sheep, "We haven't had dinner. These sheep will be sufficient for us!" Faced with no other option, Haiwa went along with the soldiers.

After the sun set, the Japanese troops stopped at a small village. They killed several sheep and ate the roasted mutton. Haiwa had no time to feel sorry for his sheep. Instead he checked beneath the old sheep's tail and was relieved to find that the letter was still there. The Japanese soldiers ate to their fill and went to sleep. The Chinese puppet soldier ordered Haiwa to herd his sheep into the sheep pen and then dragged him inside the house. The Japanese soldiers and Chinese puppet soldiers slept on the hay, holding tightly to their guns and Haiwa was placed in the innermost area.

Haiwa was unable to fall asleep. He thought, "The Japanese soldiers will slaughter more sheep tomorrow. If I can't escape tonight, they will soon find the letter." As the rooster crowed in the distance, Haiwa could no longer lie still on the ground. He sat up and saw that the guard at the door had fallen

asleep. Standing up quietly, he moved quickly to the door. He gently stepped over the guard's leg and sneaked to the sheep pen. Catching hold of the old sheep, Haiwa removed the letter from beneath its tail. He put the letter in his pocket and ran all the way up the hill.

By dawn, Haiwa had already climbed up the hilltop. He heard someone calling out ahead of him and looked up. A Japanese soldier on the other side was holding a white flag and waving at him. Haiwa took off his white shirt and imitating the Japanese soldier, he waved back. It worked and Haiwa was allowed to pass. Haiwa ran down the hill and up the hill opposite. The Wang Village was just ahead. Haiwa was delighted and sat down to rest. He put his hand inside his pocket but to his dismay, there was nothing there. Where was the letter? Trembling, Haiwa quickly removed his shirt and checked it carefully. The letter was definitely not there. He looked into all the cracks in the rocks around him but he still could not locate the letter. Haiwa immediately retraced his tracks. He climbed all the way up the hill again and at the hilltop, the very spot where he had waved his shirt earlier, he saw the letter at last, lying on the ground. Haiwa was thrilled. He put the letter in his pocket and was just about to leave when he heard someone shouting at him. It was the Chinese puppet soldier. Catching hold of Haiwa, the soldier forced him to return to lead the way for the Japanese soldiers.

The moustached soldier wielded his sword and the Japanese troops, together with the Chinese puppet soldier, set off again. Haiwa, who was to herd his sheep, was wedged in the middle. The group came to a ravine and the Wang Village was just on top of the hill in front of them. Haiwa noticed that the tree on top of the hill had fallen, a sign that Militia Commander Zhang already knew that the enemies had arrived. But the Japanese soldiers were unaware of this. They sat down to rest, drink, and smoke.

When they had rested enough, a group of Chinese puppet soldiers set off first, going up toward the hilltop. Suddenly, loud sounds and black smoke were seen from the hillside, indicating that the Chinese puppet soldiers had stepped on landmines. The moustached soldier pointed at the road ahead and said to Haiwa, "You go first and we'll follow behind. Do you understand?" Haiwa walked far ahead of the soldiers. There was a forest on the hillside which had a fork in the path. One path was for people and the other was for sheep. Haiwa drove his herd onto the latter. The Chinese puppet soldier shouted from behind, "That's the wrong path!" Haiwa shouted back, "No, it's not. I know my way. Just follow me!" The road became more and more difficult to navigate; the Japanese soldiers began to lag behind. The soldier became suspicious and shouted at Haiwa, "Slow down!" Haiwa, however, pretended not to hear him and stepped up his pace. The Japanese soldiers yelled, "Freeze, or I'll shoot!" Haiwa ignored the order. Instead, he whipped the sheep and ran even faster. The Japanese soldiers fired. Haiwa continued to run until he could no longer stand. Then he fell onto the grass, shouting, "The Japanese soldiers are coming. Shoot! Shoot at them!" All of a sudden, shots were heard from the hilltop. Upon hearing them, Haiwa knew they were from his own people...

When Haiwa opened his eyes again, he saw Commander Zhang beside him. Commander Zhang asked in concern, "Does it hurt?" Ignoring the question, Haiwa said, "The letter...The urgent letter..." The commander laughed. Putting his hand on Haiwa's head, he said, "Don't worry. I got the message. You led the Japanese soldiers to a dead end and our troops wiped them out. Thank you, you're our little hero."

(Excerpted and Abbreviated from *The Letter with Feathers*)

第六課

木蘭辭[1]

唧唧復唧唧，木蘭當戶織。不聞機杼聲，唯聞女嘆息。

問女何所思？問女何所憶？女亦無所思，女亦無所憶。

昨夜見軍帖，可汗大點兵。軍書十二卷，卷卷有爺名。

阿爺無大兒，木蘭無長兄，願為市鞍馬，從此替爺征。

王宜珈 畫

---

[1] 辭——中國古代一種文體。

東市買駿馬，西市買鞍韉，南市買轡頭，北市買長鞭。

朝辭爺娘去，暮宿黃河邊。

不聞爺娘喚女聲，但聞黃河流水鳴濺濺。

旦辭黃河去，暮宿黑山頭。

不聞爺娘喚女聲，但聞燕山胡騎聲啾啾。

萬里赴戎機，關山度若飛。朔氣傳金柝，寒光照鐵衣。

將軍百戰死，壯士十年歸。

歸來見天子，天子坐明堂。

策勳十二轉，賞賜百千強。

可汗問所欲，"木蘭不用尚書郎，

願借千里足，送兒還故鄉。"

爺娘聞女來，出郭相扶將。

阿姊聞妹來，當戶理紅妝。

小弟聞姊來，磨刀霍霍向豬羊。

開我東閣門，坐我西閣床。脫我戰時袍，著我舊時裳。

當窗理雲鬢，對鏡貼花黃。出門看伙伴，伙伴皆驚惶。

同行十二年，不知木蘭是女郎。

雄兔腳撲朔，雌兔眼迷離。

雙兔傍地走，安能辨我是雄雌。

【注釋】

機杼：織布的梭子（suō）。

可汗：古代蒙古等民族對大王的稱呼，這裏指當時的皇帝。

鞍韉：馬鞍和馬鞍下面的墊子（diàn）。

轡頭：馬嚼子（jiáo）和韁繩（jiāng）。

胡騎：胡，古代指西北的少數民族。騎，騎兵。

赴戎機：赴，去；戎，軍事。赴戎機，去打仗。

朔氣：朔，指北方。朔氣，北方的寒氣。

金柝：古代軍隊用的銅器，白天用來煮飯，晚上用來報時。

天子：皇帝。

策勳：策，古代寫字用的竹片；勳，功勞。策勳，在功勞簿（bù）上記下功勞。

賞賜：指地位高的人或長輩（bèi）把財物送給地位低的人或晚輩，表示獎勵（jiǎng lì）。

尚書：古代高官的名稱。

郭：中國古代在城的外圍加築的一道牆。

著：讀zhuó，穿。

裳：這裏讀作cháng，古音，指裙子。現在多與"衣"合用，讀作shang。

伙伴：原作"火伴"，古代兵制十人為一火，一起吃飯的人稱為"火伴"，現指一起參加活動的人。"伙伴"今也寫作"夥伴"。

撲朔：亂動。

迷離：眼神不定的樣子。

傍地走：一起在地上跑。

中國文學欣賞

生詞

wéi 唯	only		shǎng cì 賞賜	reward
yì 亦	also; too		yù 欲	want
jūn tiě 軍帖	military announcement		zǐ 姊	elder sister
ān 鞍	saddle		gé 閣	chamber; room
jùn mǎ 駿馬	steed		yī shang (衣)裳	apparel; garments
mù 暮	evening; sunset		tiē 貼	stick; adorn
sù 宿	stay overnight		huǒ bàn 伙(夥)伴	companion
dàn 旦	daybreak		jiē 皆	all
fù 赴	go to		jīng huáng 驚惶	be astounded
ruò 若	as if		nǚ láng 女郎	girl
shuò qì 朔氣	northern air		cí 雌	female
cè xūn 策勳	grant a merit		biàn bié 辨(別)	differentiate

聽寫

唯　赴　暮　若　衣裳　伙伴　貼　女郎　旦　欲

宿　皆　*雌　鞍

比一比

$$\begin{cases}若（若是）\\ 苦（痛苦）\end{cases} \quad \begin{cases}憶（記憶）\\ 億（一億）\end{cases} \quad 憶\begin{cases}回憶\\ 記憶\end{cases} \quad \begin{cases}旦（一旦）\\ 但（但是）\end{cases}$$

$$\begin{cases}裳（衣裳）\\ 賞（賞賜）\end{cases} \quad \begin{cases}賜（賞賜）\\ 易（容易）\end{cases} \quad 卷\begin{cases}第一卷\\ 考卷\end{cases} \quad \begin{cases}辯（爭辯）\\ 辨（辨別）\end{cases}$$

詞語運用

辨別

好獵人能辨別出不同動物的腳印。

你靠看星星能辨別出方向嗎？

唯有　唯一

大家都回家了，唯有他還在教室裏讀書。

他是我們班裏唯一會說德語的同學。

雌　雄

雄雞就是公雞。

玉米的雄花和雌花都長在同一株上。

找出同義、近義詞

姊　辨認　去　好馬　晚上　早晨　雌　雄

辨別（　）　赴（　）　公（　）　駿馬（　）

姐（　）　旦（　）　母（　）　暮（　）

反義詞

朝──暮　　　貼──揭　　　歸來──離去

賞──罰

詞語解釋

嘆息──嘆氣。

伙伴──指一起參加活動的人。

女郎──年輕女子。

 English Translation

Lesson Six

The Ballad of Mulan

Click, click, click,
As Mulan weaved, facing the door.
No sound of the shuttle could be heard,
But only the sighs of the girl.
What she was pondering over,
What was on her mind?
She pondered over nothing,
Nothing was on her mind.
She saw the military announcement last night,
About the Khan mustering a mighty army.
There were twelve scrolls of names,
And Father's name was in every one of them.
But Father had no son,
Mulan had no elder brother.
She wanted to buy a saddle and horse,
And serve in her Father's place.
So she bought a steed in the east market,
And a saddle in the west;
A bridle in the south market,
And a long whip in the north.
She bid farewell to her parents at dawn,
And camped by the Yellow River in the evening.
She could no longer heard her parents' calling,
She heard only the splashing of the waters.
She left the Yellow River at daybreak,
And arrived at the Black Mountain at sunset.
She could no longer heard her parents' calling,
And heard only the neighing of the horses at Mount Yan.
She traveled ten thousand miles to do battle,

She crossed mountain passes as though she was flying.
Night watches rattled in the chilly northern air,
The cold light shined down on her armor.
Generals laid down their lives in a hundred battles,
And valiant soldiers returned after ten years.
Upon her return, she saw the Emperor,
Who sat in the Hall of Brightness.
He granted her a promotion of twelve ranks,
And a reward that amounted to a hundred thousand and more.
The Khan asked her what she desired.
She replied, "I don't need any high official post,
I only want borrow a swift camel,
To take me back to my home."
When her parents heard that their daughter had returned,
They went outside the village wall to meet her, each helping the other as they went.
When her elder sister heard that her younger sister was coming,
She decked herself out in her best by the door.
When her younger brother heard that his elder sister was coming,
He whetted a knife to slaughter a pig and a sheep.
She opened the door to her east chamber,
And sat on the bed in her west chamber.
She took off her armor,
And put on the apparel she had worn of old.
Facing the window, she combed and tied up her hair,
And looked in the mirror as she adorned her hair with a yellow flower.
She went out to meet her companions,
And they were all astounded.
They had been in the army together for twelve years,
Yet none of them knew that Mulan was a girl.
Mulan said, "The male hare hops and runs,
The eyes of the female hare are blurred.
But when they run side by side in the field,
How does one tell the male from the female?"

第七課

將 相 和

戰國時期，秦國軍事實力很強，常常進攻別的國家。

有一回，趙王得了一塊珍貴的寶玉——和氏璧。秦王知道後就寫了一封信給趙王，說願意拿出十五座城來交換這塊寶玉。

趙王接到信非常著急，馬上找大臣們商議。大家都說秦王不過是想用這個法子把寶玉騙到手，不能上他的當；可是不答應，又怕他派兵來進攻。

正在為難的時候，有人說藺相如勇敢、機智，也許有辦法解決這個難題。

趙王把藺相如找來，問他怎麼辦。藺相如想了一會兒，說："我願意帶著寶玉到秦國去。如果秦王真拿十五座城來換，我就把寶玉交給他；如果他不交城，我一定會把玉帶回來。這樣一來，秦國理屈，就沒有出兵的理由了。"

藺相如來到秦國，將寶玉獻給了秦王。秦王雙手捧著寶玉，左看右看，一邊看一邊稱讚，但就是不提交城換璧的事。藺相如看出秦王並無真心，就上前一步說："大王，這塊寶玉有點兒小毛病，讓我指給您看。"秦王聽他這麼一說，就把寶玉交給了他。藺相如接過寶玉，往後退了幾步，站在柱子旁邊。他理直氣壯地說："我看您並不想交出十五座城，所以把寶玉拿了回來。您要是強逼我，我的腦袋和寶玉就一塊兒撞碎在這柱子上！"說著，舉起寶玉就要向柱子上撞。秦王怕撞碎了寶玉，連忙把他勸住，並說一切都好商量，還叫人拿出地圖，把給趙國的十五座城指給他看。藺相如又說，和氏璧是無價之寶，必須要舉行一個隆重的典禮，他纔肯交出來。秦王只好跟他約定了舉行典禮的日期。

藺相如回到賓館，就叫手下人帶著寶玉偷偷地先回趙國去了。到了典禮那一天，藺相如見了秦王，大大方方地說："寶玉已經送回趙國去了，請先把十五座城交給我國，我國馬上就會把和氏璧送來。不然，您殺了我也沒有用。"秦王沒有辦法，只得客客氣氣地送藺相如回國。

因為藺相如完璧歸趙，立了功，趙王封他做上大夫。

過了幾年，秦王約趙王在澠池①會見。趙王和大臣們商量：去，怕有危險；不去，表示膽怯。大家一時決定不了。藺相如認為不能對秦王示弱，還是去的好。趙王這纔決定動身，讓藺相如隨行。大將軍廉頗帶著軍隊送到邊界，做好了抵抗秦兵的準備。

趙王到了澠池，會見了秦王。秦王要趙王鼓瑟②。趙王不好推辭，鼓了一段。秦王就叫人記錄下來，說：在澠池會上，趙王為秦王鼓瑟。藺相如看秦王這樣侮辱趙王，生氣極了。他走到秦王面前說："請您為趙王擊缶③。"秦王不肯。藺相如說："我和您只有五步的距離。您要是不答應，我就跟您拼了！"秦王被逼得沒法，只好拿起棍來擊了幾下。藺相如也叫人記下來，說：在澠池會上，秦王為趙王擊缶。

在澠池會上，秦王沒有佔到便宜，他知道廉頗帶兵守在邊界上，也不敢把趙王怎麼樣，只好放趙王回去了。

藺相如在澠池會上又立了一功。趙王封藺相如做上卿，職位比廉頗高。廉頗知道了，不服氣地說："我為趙國打仗，立下了多少大功！可是他藺相如就靠一張嘴，竟然爬到我頭上去了！"

---

① 澠池——地名，在現今河南省澠池縣西。
② 瑟——古代一種撥弦樂器。
③ 缶——古代一種瓦質打擊樂器。

這話傳到藺相如耳朵裏。藺相如就向趙王請了病假，不再上朝，避免跟廉頗見面。

一天，藺相如坐車出去，遠遠看見廉頗騎著高頭大馬過來了，他就叫車夫把車調個頭往回趕。藺相如手下的人可看不下去了。幹什麼怕他呢！藺相如對他們說："諸位請想一想，廉將軍和秦王誰厲害？"他們回答："當然秦王厲害！"藺相如說："我連秦王都不怕，我會怕廉將軍嗎？大家知道，秦國不敢進攻我們趙國，就因為趙國武有廉頗，文有藺相如。如果我們兩個鬧彆扭，不團結，秦國就會來打我們了。"

藺相如的話傳到了廉頗的耳朵裏。廉頗覺得自己真是不應該。他脫下戰袍，背上荊條①，親自到藺相如府②上請罪。藺相如見廉頗來負荊請罪，連忙熱情地出來迎接。從此以後，他們兩個人成了好朋友，同心協力保衛趙國。

（根據司馬遷著《史記·廉頗藺相如列傳》改編）

作品簡介

《史記》是中國第一部紀傳體通史。《史記》是以人物為中心的史書，又是一部優秀的文學作品。作者司馬遷（前145—前87）是西漢時期的史學家。

---

① 荊條——一種植物的枝條，常用於編筐，古代也被用來打人。
② 府——指高官的住所。

生詞

hé shì bì 和氏璧	Heshi Jade (氏：*family name*; 璧：*jade*)	dà fang 大方	well-poised
		kè qi 客氣	polite
jī zhì 機智	quick-witted	dǎn qiè 膽怯	timid
lǐ qū 理屈	be in the wrong; have a weak case	dǐ kàng 抵抗	resist
		jī 擊	beat
pěng zhe 捧著	hold in both hands	zhàn pián yi 佔便宜	take advantage of
chēng zàn 稱讚	praise	zhí wèi 職位	position
lóng zhòng 隆重	solemn; grand	bì miǎn 避免	avoid
yuē 約	make an appointment	zhū wèi 諸位	everybody
diǎn lǐ 典禮	ceremony	jīng tiáo 荊條	brambles
bīn guǎn 賓館	guesthouse	tóng xīn xié lì 同心協力	pull together (協：*cooperate*)

聽寫

屈　捧　典禮　賓館　膽怯　抵抗　擊　職位　避免

客氣　佔便宜　機智　*隆重　稱讚

比一比

賓 { 賓館 / 賓客

典 { 典禮 / 字典

捧（捧著）/ 棒（棒子）

商 { 商議 / 商業

位 { 職位 / 諸位

璧（和氏璧）/ 壁（牆壁）

詞語運用

賓館

他到賓館去看望老朋友。

典禮

我請爸爸媽媽參加我們的高中畢業典禮。

約

小麗約小明星期日一塊兒去爬山。

找出近義詞

商量　躲開　誇　原因

商議（　　）　理由（　　）　稱讚（　　）　避開（　　）

反義詞

進攻——防守　　勇敢——膽怯　　吃虧——佔便宜

回答問題

1. 趙王得到的珍貴的寶玉叫什麼名字？

2. 秦王真的想用十五座城換這塊寶玉嗎？

3. 藺相如用什麼辦法保住了寶玉？

4. 藺相如害怕廉頗嗎？他為什麼躲避廉頗？

5. 你認為藺相如做得對不對？

6. 想一想，本課的題目《將相和》是什麼意思？

詞語解釋

同心協力——團結一心，共同努力。

理直氣壯——覺得自己有理，態度強硬。

負荊請罪——表示認錯，賠禮道歉。

完璧歸趙——比喻原物完整無損地歸還本人。

理由——原因。

相配詞連線

解決　　　秦兵

保衛　　　難題

舉行　　　祖國

抵抗　　　典禮

Lesson Seven

Friends Again: The Premier and The General

During the Warring States Period, the state of Qin had a very powerful military and often launched attacks on other states.

One day, the King of Zhao acquired the Heshi Jade which was known to be a precious piece of jade. When the King of Qin knew about it, he wrote a letter to the King of Zhao, saying that he was willing to offer 15 cities in exchange for the priceless stone.

Upon receiving of the letter, the King of Zhao grew worried and immediately summoned his ministers for a discussion. Everyone agreed that the offer from the King of Qin was a deception; he was only trying to get his hands on the precious jade and they must not fall for his ploy. However, they were afraid that he would attack if they did not comply.

Just then, someone suggested that Lin Xiangru, a brave and quick-witted man, might be able to resolve the difficult situation.

The King of Zhao sent for Lin and sought his advice. After some thought, Lin said, "Allow me, Your Majesty, to visit the State of Qin with the precious jade. If the King of Qin genuinely offers 15 cities in exchange for the jade, I will leave it with him. If not, I'll definitely bring it back with me. Then he would be unable to justify the dispatch of troops against us."

Lin arrived at the state of Qin and presented the king with the priceless stone. The king held it with both his hands and examined it admiringly. But he kept quiet about his offer. Seeing that the king was not sincere about his proposition, Lin went up to him and said, "Your Majesty, allow me to point out to you a tiny flaw in this piece of jade." After getting the jade back from the king, Lin moved backward and stood beside a pillar. He told the king boldly, "It seems as if you are not going to give us the 15 cities like what you promised so I'm taking the jade back. If you use force on me, I will smash both my head and the jade against this pillar." Holding up the precious stone, Lin was about to hit it against the pillar but the king, afraid of seeing the jade ruined, immediately urged him to stop. Assuring Lin that there was room for negotiation, the king ordered his men to bring forth a map. The king pointed out the 15 cities he was willing to give to the state of Zhao. Lin then explained that because the jade was priceless, he would not give it to the king unless a grand ceremony was held. The king had no alternative but to fix a date for the ceremony.

As soon as he retired to the guesthouse, Lin got one of his men to take the jade back secretly to the state of Zhao. On the day of the ceremony, he addressed the king confidently, saying, "The precious jade has been sent back to my home state. Please yield the 15 cities to us first, and we will send you the jade in return. Otherwise, killing me wouldn't change anything!" The king relented and saw Lin off politely.

Because Lin returned the jade intact, the King of Zhao promoted him to a high-ranking official.

A few years later, the King of Qin invited the King of Zhao to a meeting at Mianchi. The King of Zhao discussed the matter with his ministers as accepting the invitation could pose a danger to the king, but declining it might imply that he was timid. No one could come to a decision. Lin felt that the King of Zhao should go for the meeting lest the King of Qin interpreted the refusal as a sign of weakness. The King of Zhao finally decided to set off, with Lin accompanying him. The great general Lian Po sent them to the borders, bringing with him his troops, prepared to resist any invasion from the army of Qin.

The two kings met at Mianchi. When the host, the King of Qin, invited his counterpart to play the se (a string instrument) at the party, the King of Zhao could not decline and had to oblige. The King of Qin then instructed his men to make a record of the playing so as to give the idea that the King of Zhao had entertained him at Mianchi by performing the se. Feeling angry at the insult, Lin approached the King of Qin, saying "Now please play a tune with the fou (a percussion instrument) for my king in return." The King of Qin refused and Lin said, "There are only five steps between you and me. If you don't do as I say, I will fight it out with you, even if it means risking my life. " Helpless, the King of Qin gave his performance. Lin then told his men to note down these words, "The King of Qin played a tune for the King of Zhao at a party held in Mianchi."

Because of this, the King of Qin failed to take advantage of the King of Zhao at Mianchi. He knew that General Lian Po and his men were stationed near the border, so he had no choice but to let his guests go.

Having once again succeeded in his task, Lin was made the premier of the state, a position even higher than that of General Lian Po's. When the latter learned about this, he was offended and said, "I've fought hard for the state of Zhao and done much to safeguard it. Yet, Lin Xiangru, a glib talker, has had such a meteoric rise above me!" When Lin caught wind of this, he claimed that he was sick to avoid going to court, so that he and Lian Po would not run into one another.

One day, Lin was going down the streets in his chariot when he saw Lian Po, high on horseback, approaching him. Lin told his driver to turn back. His courtiers began to complain, "Why should we be afraid of Lian Po?" Lin asked them, "Tell me, who is more formidable: General Lian or the King

of Qin?" They answered, "Surely, the King of Qin." Lin continued, "You are right. But if I'm not even afraid of the King of Qin, would I be afraid of General Lian? As you know, the army of Qin has not dared to attack us because they know that General Lian and I are working together to safeguard our state. If we are at odds with each other, the troops from Qin will surely attack us."

When this was related to General Lian, he felt ashamed. Taking off his armor, he strapped brambles to his bare back and walked to Lin's house to ask for his forgiveness. Lin came out to receive him warmly. From then on, the two men became good friends and worked together to safeguard the state of Zhao.

(Adapted from *The Historical Records* by Sima Qian, Translated by Xiong Wenhua)

第八課

考 試

上課了，教語文的陳老師走進了高一（4）班，手裏拿著考卷說："開學到現在已有兩個星期了。今天進行一次考試，桌面除了筆，其他東西都收起來！""又搞突然襲擊！完了完了，死定了！"有人叫著。但是卷子一到手，便只有春蠶進食的聲音了。陳老師出的卷子總是滿滿當當，不抓緊時間很難做完，埋頭作答是正道。

不過，半個小時後，有些人開始活動了。余發首先想到的救兵是王笑天。他偷偷地看了老師一眼：老師望著窗外，好像在看什麼。余發放心了，將問題寫在小紙條上，揉成一團扔給最後一排的王笑天。就在這時，老師轉過身來，巧的是紙團不偏不倚正好落在後面的垃圾桶裏。老師皺了一下眉，沒有言語，低頭改作業。余發連忙又

Uta Guo 畫

扔了一個紙團過去。老師走下去拾起來，一看是張白紙，說了句"上課不要亂扔垃圾"就又回到講臺。

作弊雖然不成，但是也沒被老師抓著，余發暗自得意："老師怎麼鬥得過學生！"不過余發不敢再作弊了。陳老師看起來在改作業，實際上是一心兩用。她不時用眼睛掃描全班。遞條子、翻書、偷看都不行，余發只能硬著頭皮自己做了。

答考卷先易後難，余發當然懂，但是找來找去，找不到一道題是容易的！看來只能撞大運了，撞好了，也許能及格呢。余發坐直身子，伸出左手，四個手指代表ABCD，心中默念兒歌，目光隨著兒歌的節拍數著左手指。兒歌結束時，目光停止在哪個指頭上，就把它的編號填到選擇題上。老師從高處往下看，看到的是余發用心思考、認真書寫的情景。

一位同學站起來："老師，請多給一張紙。"

他叫陳明，頭髮有點兒亂，不知是獨特的髮型，還是不梳頭的結果。他是這個班的學習委員，是個……用現今校園裏最流行的詞來說是"Cool"。

老師拿了張白紙從講臺上走下來，看了看陳明的卷子，臉上浮現出了笑容。所有的人都抬起眼睛看著陳明，那目光有讚歎，有妒忌：這家伙又要"獨領風騷（são）"了！

這時謝欣然正在想《長江三日》的作者是誰，考前明明還看過這一課，怎麼這會兒全糊塗了呢？這是怎麼啦？

慌亂中欣然回頭看看蕭遙。他正在答題。考試前，誰都說"我沒看書啊"，"我沒背啊"，可是真考起來，一個比一個答得快，答得多。看來，中學生也夠虛偽的。

下課了。"收卷吧，到時間了。"

欣然把卷子交上去。老師一邊整理卷子，一邊對欣然說："上次小考你就退步了，成績不如以前。怎麼，好像有什麼心事？""沒……沒有。"

"沒有就好。女孩子大了心容易散，不要認為自己不錯就放鬆。"

欣然心想：我哪兒敢放鬆啊，一天恨不得有32小時纔好。

"同學們都坐好了！和大家說一件事。這是我最後一次給你們考試，我要住院開刀去了，以後出院也不能再帶你們了。從下星期起，江老師教你們，他教學經驗十分豐富。我還是那句老話：對自己不要放鬆。下課！"

"老師，您得了什麼病啊？"一位長得很出眾的女孩子站了起來，她叫劉夏。"老師，您在哪家醫院治病啊？"女孩子們七嘴八舌地問。

陳老師顯然很激動："也沒什麼大病。年紀大了，病也多了。你們好好學習就是對老師最好的安慰。"

同學們這纔三三兩兩地離開教室。

欣然站在路邊，心裏想，平時考試都很好，但是這回……難道是因為他？欣然倒吸了幾口冷氣。

這時，她看見王笑天、蕭遙在打籃球，心一下子熱了起來。

王笑天是校籃球隊的主力隊員，是個"小帥哥"，雖然臉上有幾顆"星星點燈"似的青春痘（dòu），卻不影響他在不少女生心目中"白馬王子"的地位。他籃球打得好。每次比賽，王笑天那漂亮的帶球過人三步上籃，定能引起喝（hè）彩。每當這時，王笑天便衝著球迷們揚揚拳頭，頭髮往後一甩——他還真當自己是喬丹①了。這更讓那些球迷興奮。

不隱瞞地說，九中不少女生背後悄悄地給王笑天打過100分。可欣然認為男孩子光是英俊是不行的，還要有能力、有才氣、性格好。她心目中也有打滿分的人，那就是蕭遙。

蕭遙是他們的班長，父母在國外工作，蕭遙和爺爺奶奶住在深圳（zhèn）②。

才華和英俊的相貌相比，女孩子們更容易偏向才華。欣然覺得自己的那份情是淡淡的、淺淺的，但是並不輕鬆……這種感覺她是絕對不會對別人說的，何況也說不清楚。

欣然望著蕭遙的背影，若有所思。

（根據郁秀著《花季雨季》選段改編）

---

① 喬丹——美國著名的前籃球運動員。

② 深圳——地名，位於中國廣東省。

生詞

chén 陳	Chen (surname)	fà xíng 髮型	hair style
gǎo 搞	do; be engaged in	shū tóu 梳頭	comb one's hair
xí jī 襲擊	a surprise attack	wěi yuán 委員	committee member
yú 余	Yu (surname)	liú xíng 流行	popular
róu 揉	crumple into a ball	xiāo 蕭	Xiao (surname)
bù piān bù yǐ 不偏不倚	balanced	xū wěi 虛偽	hypocritical
zhòu méi 皺眉	frown	chéng jì 成績	grades; result
zuò bì 作弊	cheat	jī dòng 激動	excited; agitated
shí jì shang 實際上	actually; in reality	shuài gē 帥哥	handsome boy
sǎo miáo 掃描	scan	qiáo dān 喬丹	Michael Jordan
dì 遞	hand over; pass	xīng fèn 興奮	excited
yìng zhe tóu pí 硬著頭皮	brace oneself	yǐn mán 隱瞞	conceal; hide
jí gé 及格	pass a test	yīng jùn 英俊	handsome
jié shù 結束	end; finish	qiǎn 淺	subtle; shallow
xuǎn zé 選擇	choice	jué duì 絕對	absolute

聽寫

陳　眉　遞　選擇　激動　帥　及格　英俊　成績　淺

余　喬　結束　*委員　隱瞞

比一比

```
⎧ 柔（柔和）    ⎧ 俊（英俊）    ⎧ 真（真假）    ⎧ 童（兒童）
⎨                ⎨                ⎨                ⎨
⎩ 揉（揉成）    ⎩ 駿（駿馬）    ⎩ 填（填寫）    ⎩ 撞（撞大運）

⎧ 為（為了）    ⎧ 帥（帥哥）    ⎧ 滿（滿意）    ⎧ 恨（恨不得）
⎨                ⎨                ⎨                ⎨
⎩ 偽（虛偽）    ⎩ 師（老師）    ⎩ 瞞（隱瞞）    ⎩ 很（很好）
```

詞語運用

流行

去年服裝的流行色是黑色，今年流行什麼顏色？

你喜歡唱流行歌曲嗎？

選擇

飛機上的午餐只有雞肉飯和牛肉面兩種選擇。

哥哥上了大學，他選擇了化學專業。

反義詞

抓緊——放鬆　　進步——退步　　輕鬆——沉重

公開——秘密　　激動——平靜　　虛偽——真誠

開始——結束　　深——淺

多音字

興 xīng
興奮 xīng

興 xìng
高興 xìng

散 sǎn
鬆散 sǎn

散 sàn
霧散了 sàn

回答問題

1. 余發學習好嗎?

2. 余發想到的救兵是誰?

3. 余發作弊成功了嗎?

4. 最後余發是怎樣答考卷的?

5. 班裏學習最好的人是誰?

6. 不少女生心中的"白馬王子"是誰?

7. 男生的才華和英俊相比，欣然更偏向哪一個?

詞語解釋

喝彩——大聲叫好。

不時——經常、不斷地。

何況——再說。

若有所思——好像在想什麼。

讚歎——誇、稱讚。

獨領風騷——一個人領先於大家,也就是說他的成績比別人都好。

相配詞連線

用心　　　　時間

抓緊　　　　歌曲

流行　　　　思考

Lesson Eight

The Test

It was time for class and Ms. Chen, the Chinese teacher, entered the classroom of Class 4, Senior Grade 1, with a set of test papers in her hands. "It's been two weeks since the start of term. Today, we'll have a test. Clear your desks. Only pens are allowed on them!" "Oh no, a pop quiz again. I'm dead!" someone shouted. But once the paper had been distributed to everyone, there was only the sound of pens writing on paper, like that of spring silkworms eating mulberry leaves. Test papers set by Ms. Chen were always full of questions and no one could afford to waste time. The students started to answer the questions immediately.

After half an hour, some of the students began to fidget. The first person Yu Fa wanted to turn to for help was Wang Xiaotian. He stole a quick glance at the teacher who was looking out the window at something. Feeling relieved, Yu Fa wrote his question on a small piece of paper. He kneaded it into a ball and threw it at Wang Xiaotian who was sitting in the last row. Just at that moment, the teacher turned around. Coincidentally, the ball of paper fell into the trash can at the back of the classroom. The teacher frowned a little and continued correcting the students' homework without saying anything. Yu Fa immediately threw out a second ball of paper. This time, the teacher walked over and picked it up. Seeing that it was a piece of blank paper, she said to the class, "Don't throw garbage in class." Then she returned to her desk.

Although he did not succeeded in cheating, Yu Fa had not been caught by the teacher either. He was proud of himself and thought, "How can a teacher possibly triumph over a student!" But Yu Fa dared not cheat now. Although Ms. Chen seemed to be correcting their homework, her eyes were actually scanning the entire class. It was impossible to pass any notes, look at any textbooks, or peek at others' answer sheet. Yu Fa braced himself to answer the questions entirely on his own.

Yu Fa knew that easy questions in a test usually came before the difficult ones. But after looking through all the questions, he could not find one easy question! He then decided to count on his luck. If he was lucky enough, he just might pass the test. Yu Fa sat up and stretched out his left hand. With the four fingers representing A, B, C, and D, Yu Fa chanted a nursery rhyme quietly. He moved his eyes along the fingers, counting them according to the rhythm. Whichever finger the rhyme ended on, he would write the corresponding letter down on the answer sheet. What Ms. Chen would see would be a serious Yu Fa thinking carefully and writing earnestly on his paper.

One student stood up and said, "Teacher, please give me another piece of paper."

It was Chen Ming, the student with slightly messy hair. No one could tell whether his hair was meant to be a unique hairstyle or if it was merely the result of not combing his hair. He was the committee member in charge of study matters in the class and was regarded as the definition of "cool" by the entire campus.

Ms. Chen took a piece of blank paper and walked down from the platform. She looked at Chen Ming's answer sheet and smiled satisfactorily. Everyone looked at Chen Ming, some with admiration and some with jealousy, "That guy has it all!"

At this time, Xie Xinran was thinking hard about the name of the author of Three Days over the Yangtze River. "I reviewed the lesson just before the test. Why can't I remember a thing now? What is wrong with me?" she thought.

In her panic, Xiran turned around and looked at Xiao Yao. He was answering the questions. Before the test, everyone had claimed "I haven't reviewed my lesson," or "I didn't memorize a thing." But when the test began, they all bent over and answered quickly. It seemed that most high school students were hypocritical.

The bell rang. Ms. Chen said, "OK, time's up. Please hand in your papers."

Xinran handed up her paper. As Ms Chen put the papers in order, she said to Xinran, "Your grades have deteriorated since the last quiz. Is there anything wrong? Do you have any concerns on your mind?" Xinran replied, "Concerns? N... no."

"That's good. When a girl grows up, her mind tends to go wild. Don't slacken by thinking that you're good enough."

Xinran thought, "I wouldn't dare to slacken. In fact, I wish there were 32 hours a day."

"Students, please return to your seats. I have something to tell you. This is my last pop quiz for you. I'll be going for an operation and will no longer be your teacher even after I am discharged. From next week on, Mr. Jiang will be your teacher. He is an experienced teacher. My last words to you are these 'Do not slacken in your efforts.' OK, class is over!"

A good-looking girl, Liu Xia, stood up and asked, "Ms. Chen, what kind of illness do you have?" "Ms. Chen, which hospital are you going to for treatment?" All the girls began to talk at once.

Obviously agitated, Ms. Chen said, "It's not a big deal. When one grows old, illness will follow. Study hard, that's the best you can do for me."

The students then left the classroom in twos and threes.

Xinran stood by the roadside, thinking, "I used to do well in the tests, but this time... Is this all because of him?" She shuddered a little at this.

Just at that moment, she saw Wang Xiaotian and Xiao Yao playing basketball and her heart warmed.

Wang Xiaotian was the main player in the school's basketball team. He was handsome even though he had some pimples on his face. Many young girls still thought of them as their Prince Charming. He played basketball well. In every match, his skillful shooting would always earn him lots of cheers. At moments like that, Xiaotian would wave his fists at the fans and throw his head backward, flinging his hair back—he really regards himself as Michael Jordan. This would inevitably excite the fans even more.

It was not a secret that many girls in the school gave Wang Xiaotian a high score of 100 points. But Xinran felt that just being good-looking was not sufficient; a boy must also have ability, talent, and a good character. The one she awarded a perfect score to was Xiao Yao.

Xiao Yao was the class monitor. His parents worked abroad and he lived with his grandparents in Shenzhen.

Between talent and a handsome appearance, girls would prefer a boy with talent. Xinran knew her feelings were subtle but not fleeting. It was a feeling that she would never share with others, she could not explain it clearly anyway.

Xinran continued gazing at Xiao Yao pensively, thoughtful.

(Excerpted and Abbreviated from Yu Xiu's novel *Flower Season, Rainy Season*)

第九課

《卧虎藏龍》選段

　　一天,玉小姐正在房裏讀書,忽聽外面大廳傳來父親嚴厲的聲音。玉小姐見廳下跪著一個武官,樣子十分惶恐。父親生氣地說:"養兵千日,用兵一時。一百騎兵也不算少,為何銀子、武器被搶?"

　　那軍官道:"我領著百人剛進沙漠,忽見遠處起了一排黃雲。有人大叫說:'不好,半天雲來了!'話音剛落,只見馬賊飛騎來到。我們馬上迎戰,可是領頭的那個馬賊十分勇猛,官兵

遇他，非死即傷。沒多久，被他殺死打傷的弟兄已有二十多個。聽說他外號叫半天雲，可他的姓名、年齡、相貌，都沒人知道。有人說他少年英俊，一表人才，也有人說他老當益壯……"

父親退進後廳悶坐在椅子上，玉小姐悄悄退入母親房裏，安慰母親說："請母親不必擔心，一群小小馬賊算得了什麼。"

母親嘆了口氣說："聽說這半天雲可厲害啦，不能不讓人擔心呀！"

第二天一早，玉帥親自帶領精兵，出發捉馬賊。臨行前，玉小姐對父親說："父親年歲已大，難道為幾個馬賊，還要親自去嗎？"玉帥看了女兒一眼說："你一個女孩子家，懂得什麼！"

玉帥一走，玉小姐心裏一陣氣惱。她覺得這一切都是那個半天雲惹起來的。她想到城外草原上散散心，於是騎上馬，帶了兩個衛兵向城外奔去。一路上，玉小姐問："那馬賊為何叫半天雲？"衛兵說："他帶著一幫人馬，多在沙漠出沒，當他的馬隊衝過來，塵沙飛入天空，就像起了半天長雲一般，因此沙漠上的人們都稱他為半天雲。"衛兵看了玉小姐一眼，又說："別看那半天雲是個馬賊，可草原上的人都護著他呢。"

玉小姐說："他是個馬賊，專門和官家作對的了。"衛兵說："還有草原上那些地主、頭人①。"

---

① 頭人——對一些少數民族部落首領的稱呼。

進入草原，玉小姐的馬像箭一般飛跑，沒多久就把兩個衛兵遠遠拋在後面。忽然，她聽到後面有馬蹄聲響，越來越近，她不知哪兒來的快馬能趕上她。正要回頭看時，那匹馬已趕上來和她並列一起了。她一看，只見那馬上的人，年約二十來歲，粗短身材，濃眉毛，三角眼，衣飾華麗，面帶邪(xié)笑。那人死死盯著她，把她從頭到腳不住打量。玉小姐又羞又惱，抽了一馬鞭，想把那人拋在後面。不料剛跑出一個馬頭，那人又趕了上來說："哪裏飛來的小鳥，真美呀！"

　　玉小姐哪裏受過這般輕薄，順手就向那人一鞭揮去。那人將頭一伏，躲過鞭子，趁勢一伸手抓住玉小姐腰帶就拉。玉小姐一邊掙扎，一邊用鞭朝那人亂抽。二人一拉一扯，兩匹馬也慢慢停了下來。玉小姐漲紅了臉，雙目圓睜，怒喝道："你不想活了？"那人卻嘻皮笑臉地說："碰到你這樣美的人，我還想活哩(li)！告訴你，我是巴格，跟了我是你的福氣！"說著又動起手來。

　　玉小姐由怒變成了急，差點兒哭了起來。巴格只顧用力將玉小姐往自己馬上拖。玉小姐情急，趁他不防，用口在他肩上使勁一咬，只聽他"唉喲(āi yō)"一聲，忙把手縮了回去。這時，玉小姐看到他的眼裏閃著綠光的眼珠，不覺渾身打了個哆嗦。她正想逃跑，巴格又撲了過來，右手抓著玉小姐的腰帶，用力一提，便將她提離馬鞍。正在這時，忽聽得耳邊響起一陣馬蹄聲，不遠處，一匹火紅色的馬衝來，直衝到巴格面前。巴格慌得躲閃不及，跌下馬去。玉小姐抬頭一看，馬上騎著一人，頭戴一頂皮帽，遮住眉毛，身穿一件白布衫，腰上掛了一把短刀。那人生著一副壯實的身材，胸部肌肉鼓聳（sǒng），好像要裂衣而出一般。馬剛一停下，那人便用鞭子指著巴格喝道："光天化日之下，欺負一個單身弱女，你算什麼漢子！"

巴格說道："你是什麼人？敢來管我巴格的事！"那漢子說："我就是草原上專門打狼射豹的人。巴格，我勸你少作惡！"巴格惱羞成怒，氣勢洶洶地伸出手來拖那漢子，不料那漢子在馬上不退不避，讓他把腿抱住。巴格用力一拖，那漢子卻紋絲不動。巴格臉漲得通紅，脖子上的青筋鼓得老粗。那漢子任他去拖，毫不在意地說："你拉吧，再加點兒力氣，我可不是女流之輩①啊！"說完放聲大笑。巴格趁那漢子放聲笑時，偷偷拔出了腰間短刀，猛地向那漢子刺去。玉小姐在一旁看得明白，驚呼一聲："留神！"那漢子以出人意外的敏捷，一伸手就把巴格的手腕握住，用力一扭，只聽巴格一聲大叫，刀便落到地上去了。那漢子這纔轉過臉來看著玉小姐，眼神裏帶著關切說："看你不像草原上的人，這兒不是你玩兒的地方，還是回家吧。"玉小姐心裏一陣驚奇。她也就在這時纔看見了那漢子的面容：皮帽遮眉，剩下半張紫銅色的臉上，一雙閃電般的眼睛。這件事發生

---

① 女流之輩——指婦女，表示輕視的口氣。

得那樣突然，玉小姐有如在夢裏。不知為什麼，那漢子剛纔所説的一些話似乎都使她生氣。自己是一個邊帥的千金小姐，可在那大漢眼裏好像比一匹小馬都不如呢。但又不能對他發火，本來還應該謝謝他纔對呢！這時，後面馬蹄聲又響了，三人同時回頭一看，玉小姐高興地説："我的人來了。"那漢子突然眼裏閃出一種厭惡的目光。只聽他説了句："啊，原來你們都是一個廟裏的神！我纔多管閒事！"説完，向草原深處飛奔而去了。

這時，巴格也掙扎上馬，只説了句："原來你是軍營中的人，得罪！"也趕忙跑了。等兩個衛兵跑到時，玉小姐説："快追上去，把那個叫巴格的給我捉來。"

兩個衛兵停著不動，對玉小姐説："不行啊，小姐，那是格桑頭人的兒子，捉了他會惹出麻煩來的。"玉小姐生氣地説："什麼格桑頭人，難道我父親還管不著他！"衛兵説："這西疆人人都歸大帥管，只是目前出了個半天雲，就已夠大帥著急的了，像格桑那樣的人還是不去惹他的好。"

玉小姐聽了衛兵的話，心裏也明白過來，不再説什麼了。玉小姐在回城的路上，心裏想：巴格既然那麼不好惹，那漢子又為何不把他放在眼裏呢？那漢子又是個什麼樣的人呢？玉小姐好像還在夢裏。

（根據王度廬原著《臥虎藏龍》及聶雲嵐改寫本《玉嬌龍》節選改編）

生詞

wò 卧	crouch; lie down	xī pí xiào liǎn 嘻皮笑臉	grin cheekily
mǎ zéi 馬賊	mounted; bandit	jiān 肩	shoulder
yù 遇	meet	suō 縮	withdraw; pull back
wài hào 外號	nickname	shān 衫	clothes
nián líng 年齡	age	fù 副	a measure word (for faual expression, etc.)
lǎo dāng yì zhuàng 老当益壯	old but vigorous	qī fu 欺負	bully
lín xíng 臨行	just before leaving	nǎo xiū chéng nù 惱羞成怒	be shamed into anger
rě 惹	provoke	bèi 輩	people of a certain kind; generation
chén shā 塵沙	dust and sand	mǐn jié 敏捷	nimble
yì bān 一般	same as; general	shǒu wàn 手腕	wrist
zuò duì 作對	oppose	zǐ 紫	purple
dīng 盯	stare	yàn wù 厭惡	loath; hate
dǎ liang 打量	size somebody up	xián shì 閑事	other people's business

聽寫

盯　肩　欺負　怒　輩　閑　年齡　塵沙　一般　遇

衫　紫　*縮　賊

第九課

比一比

腰 { 腰帶 / 彎腰

紋 { 花紋 / 紋絲不動

拖 { 拖延 / 拖拉

負 { 負責 / 欺負

詞語運用

敏捷
擊劍運動員的動作十分敏捷。

厭惡
半天雲對官府的人十分厭惡。
人們愛好和平,厭惡戰爭。

管閒事
媽媽愛管閒事,即使不認識的人遇到困難,她也會幫忙。

老當益壯
爺爺都70歲了,一頭白髮,還參加長跑比賽,真是老當益壯。

找出近義詞

碰到　勇敢　討厭(tǎo)　年齡　小偷　面容

賊（　　）　　勇猛（　　）　　年歲（　　）

相貌（　　）　　厭惡（　　）　　遇到（　　）

反義詞

伸——縮　　　　欺負——愛護

閑——忙　　　　厭惡——喜愛

多音字

中國文學欣賞

惡 è	惡 wù
作惡 è	厭惡 wù

似 sì	似 shì
似乎 sì	像……似的 shì

回答問題

1. 官兵的銀子、武器被誰搶了？

2. 草原上的人是痛恨半天雲還是護著他？

3. 誰欺負了玉小姐？

4. 誰救了玉小姐？

5. 你認為戴皮帽的漢子可能是誰？

詞語解釋

壯實——強壯、健壯。

氣勢洶洶——形容非常生氣時很兇的樣子。

作惡——做壞事。

留神——小心。

關切——關心。

一表人才——表，相貌。形容人外貌英俊，風度自然、大方。

老當益壯——雖然年老，但更有志氣，更有勁頭。

嘻皮笑臉——形容打打鬧鬧、嘻嘻哈哈，不嚴肅的樣子。

光天化日之下——大白天，陽光下。比喻公開場合。

紋絲不動——一點也不動。

似乎——好像。

Lesson Nine

Crouching Tiger, Hidden Dragon

One day, while reading a book in her study, Miss Yu suddenly heard her father talking harshly outside. She saw a terrified military officer on his knees in the hall. "Armies are to be maintained in the course of long years but to be used in the nick of time," her father said angrily. "One hundred cavalry soldiers is not a small number. How could you have been robbed of your silver and weapons?"

The officer replied, "I had just led 100 men into the desert when we saw a yellow sandstorm in the distance. Someone shouted, 'Oh no, Bantianyun (Cloud over Half the Sky) is coming!' No sooner had he said that than bandits on horseback approached. We met the enemy head-on but their chief was so ferocious that in a short while, he had killed and wounded over 20 of our soldiers. I heard that his nickname is Bantianyun, but no one knows his real name, age, or appearance. Some say that he is a handsome young man, but others describe him as a robust old man..."

When her father had retired to the rear hall and was sitting there all alone, Miss Yu went quietly into her mother's room and comforted her, saying, "Don't worry, Mother. They're just a small gang of bandits!"

Her mother sighed and said, "I've heard that Bantianyun is a formidable man. I can't help but worry!"

The next morning, Commander Yu (Miss Yu's father) made preparations to personally lead a troop of soldiers to arrest the bandits. Just before he left, Miss Yu said, "Father, you are getting on in years. Do you really have to attend to this matter personally?" Her father gave her a hard look, saying "You girls won't understand this!"

After her father left, Miss Yu was somewhat annoyed. She felt that all this trouble was caused by one man, this Bantianyun. Wanting to go out to the prairie to relax, she mounted her horse and left the city, escorted by two guards. Along the way, Miss Yu asked them, "Why is that bandit called Bantianyun?" One of the guards replied, "He leads his men and they maneuver in and out of the desert. When his troops attack, dust and sand fly in the air and it looks like there are clouds over half the sky. That's why the local people call him Bantianyun." The guard looked at her and continued, "He may be a bandit but the herdsmen are partial to him."

Miss Yu said, "A bandit like him goes directly against the government." The guard added, "And the local landlords and chieftains as well!"

Entering the prairie, Miss Yu began to gallop across the grassland. Soon she left the two guards far behind. Suddenly, she heard the sound of a horse's hoofs behind her. The sound became louder and louder. She was wondering what horse could possibly catch up with hers but before she could turn round to find out, the horseman had already caught up with her and was riding by her side. Looking at the rider, she saw a young man who was about 20 years old. He was short and stout, with thick brows above his slit eyes. The man was elegantly dressed and had an evil smile on his face. He stared hard at her, looking her up and down. Miss Yu was very offended by his arrogance. She wielded the whip and spurred her horse on, hoping to leave the man behind. But she failed and the horseman caught up once again and rode beside her. He said, "Where did this bird come from? How beautiful it is!"

Miss Yu, who had never been subject to such frivolous behavior, retaliated by wielding her whip on him. He dodged his head to avoid the beating, and at the same time, took advantage of the position by grasping her girdle. As she struggled to free herself, she whipped him all over. Their horses gradually slowed down as a result of their fighting. Red in her face and glaring fiercely, she shouted at him, "Are you asking for death?" But the man, grinning cheekily, said, "No! I want to live as long as I can in the company of such a pretty girl. May I introduce myself? My name is Bage. You'll be happy if you stay with me." And he began to touch her again.

His reply turned her anger into panic and she was on the verge of tears. When he tried to carry her over from her horseback, she bit him hard on the shoulder when he was not on guard. He groaned loudly and immediately withdrew his hand. His eyes glistened and she trembled upon seeing them. She tried to run away but Bage threw himself on her. Holding her girdle in his right hand, he lifted her up from the saddle. Just then, she heard a clatter of horse's hoofs. A flaming red horse was making a dash at Bage. Without enough time to dodge, Bage fell off his horse. Looking up, Miss Yu saw a man on horseback. He had a fur hat covering his eyebrows and was dressed in white, with a dagger strapped around his waist. The man had a robust stature, with bulging muscles that stretched his clothes almost to the point of bursting. As soon as he came to a stop, he pointed his whip at Bage, shouting, "How dare you bully a weak girl in broad daylight! What kind of a man are you?"

Bage retorted, "Who are you? How dare you stick your nose into Bage's business!" The man said,

"You may consider me a grassland hunter who stalks wolves and leopards. Bage, I warn you to stop your wicked deeds!" Bage was shamed into anger and he tried to drag the man from his horse. The man did not dodge but allowed Bage to catch hold of his leg. No matter how hard Bage tugged, the man remained seated on his horse. In his effort to unseat the man, Bage flushed crimson and his veins stood out on his neck. The man allowed Bage to continue to tug and pull at him. He laughed scornfully and sneered, "Go on, pull! Use a little more strength. I'm not a woman, you know!" While the man was laughing, Bage stealthily drew out his dagger and tried to stab the man. Seeing Bage's intention, Miss Yu cried, "Watch out!" The man nimbly reached out and held Bage's wrist, twisting it with force. Bage cried out in pain and the dagger fell to the ground. Only then did the man turn round to behold Miss Yu. Looking at her with concern, he said, "You don't seem like a native of the grassland. This is not the place for you to have fun. You'd better go home." Miss Yu was startled when she was finally able to see him clearly. His fur hat covered his eyebrows, exposing only half of his tanned face and a pair of flashing eyes. Everything happened so quickly; it seemed like a dream. She somehow felt upset about what the man had just said. She was the daughter of a border commander. Yet in the man's eyes, she seemed no better than a pony. But she felt it inappropriate to express her anger at a time when she owed him her gratitude. Just then, they heard the sound of horses' hoofs again. All three turned round. Miss Yu said happily, "My guards are coming." With hatred flashing in his eyes, the man said, "So you are birds of the same feather! I shouldn't have minded other people's business!" With that, he raced toward the inner grassland.

Bage also struggled to mount his horse. Before riding off, he said, "Sorry! I didn't realize that you are from the barracks." When the two guards arrived, Miss Yu ordered them, "Quick, give chase. Go and arrest Bage!"

The two guards stood still, saying, "We can't, Miss. His father is the chieftain of Gesang. Getting him arrested would create trouble." Miss Yu said angrily, "Chieftain? So what? Do you think he is not under my father's jurisdiction?" The guards answered, "The people here are all under the commander's jurisdiction. But the commander already has much to worry about since the appearance of Bantianyun. We'd better leave Gesang and his men alone."

After listening to the guards, Miss Yu understood and said nothing more about it. On the way back home, she thought, "If Bage is not to be trifled with, why did the man not have any regard for him? What kind of a man is he?" Miss Yu felt as if she were in a dream.

(Adapted from a novel rewritten on the basis of the original by Wang Dulu)

第十課

黛玉與寶玉

（選學課）

　　且說黛玉自那日下船時，便有榮府的轎子等候。上了轎，進了城，從窗中看了一看，街市十分熱鬧。又行了半日，忽見街北有兩個大石獅子，三間大門，是"榮國府"。臺階上坐著幾個穿紅著(zhuó)綠的丫(yā)頭①，一見他們來了，都笑著迎上來說："林姑娘來了！"

　　黛玉方進房，只見兩個人扶著一位鬢(bìn)髮如銀的老太太迎上來。黛玉知是外祖母了，正要下拜，早被外祖母抱住，摟入懷中，"心肝兒肉"叫著，大哭起來。黛玉也哭個不休。眾人慢慢解勸，那黛玉方拜見了外祖母。

　　過了一會兒，只聽後院中有笑語聲，說："我來遲了，沒得迎接遠客！"黛玉心想："這些人個個連大氣都不敢出，這

---

① 丫頭——指年輕的女僕。

來的是誰，這樣無禮？"只見一群婦人、丫頭擁著一個麗人從後房進來。這個人衣著彩繡輝煌，美若天仙；一雙丹鳳眼，兩彎柳葉眉，身材苗條。黛玉連忙起身接見。眾姐妹都忙告訴黛玉道："這是璉二嫂子。"這熙鳳①拉著黛玉的手，上下細細打量一回，笑道："天下真有這樣漂亮的人兒！我今日纔算看見了。"又問道："妹妹幾歲了？可上過學？現吃什麼藥？在這裏別想家，要什麼吃的、什麼玩的，只管告訴我。丫頭、老婆子們不好，也只管告訴我。"黛玉一一答應著。

吃過茶，黛玉去見王夫人。王夫人說："你三個姐妹倒都極好，以後一處唸書認字，學針線，她們都會讓著你。我就只一件事不放心：我有一個'混世魔王'，今日因往廟裏去，還沒回來，晚上你看見就知道了。你以後不用理他。你這些姐姐妹妹都不敢沾惹他的。"黛玉曾經聽母親說過，有個內侄銜玉而生，不喜讀書，外祖母又溺愛，無人敢管。今見王夫人所說，便知是這位表兄，一面笑道："舅母所說，可是銜玉而生的？在家時記得母親常說，這位哥哥比我大一歲，小名就叫寶玉，性雖頑皮，但與姐妹們極好。我來了，自然和姐妹們一處，怎會去沾惹他？"王夫人笑道："你哪裏知道，他從小和姐妹們相處慣了，要是姐妹們不理他，倒還安分些；要是哪一天姐妹們和他多說了一句

---

① 熙鳳——即上文提到的璉二嫂子，名字叫王熙鳳。

話，他心上一喜，便生出許多事來。所以勸你別理他。"黛玉一一的都答應著。

賈母①問黛玉唸何書。黛玉道："剛唸了《四書》。"黛玉又問姐妹們讀何書，賈母道："讀什麼書，不過認得幾個字。"正說著，只聽外面一陣腳步響，有人說："寶玉來了。"黛玉心想，這個寶玉不知是怎樣個人呢。進來一看，卻是位青年公子②：頭戴寶石紫金冠，身穿百蝶大紅上衣；面若中秋之月，色如春曉之花，鬢若刀裁，眉如墨畫，睛若秋波；脖子上掛著一塊美玉。黛玉一見便大吃一驚，心中想道："好奇怪，倒像在哪裏見過的，何等眼熟！"只見這寶玉向賈母請了安，賈母便命："去見你娘來。"寶玉即轉身去了。再來時，已換了衣服，身上穿著銀紅花大襖，仍舊帶著寶玉，下面半露松綠花綢褲，厚底大紅鞋。天然一段風韵(yùn)情思，全在眉眼間。

賈母見他進來，笑道："還不去見你妹妹呢。"寶玉早已看見了一個秀麗的女孩兒，料定是林姑媽之女，忙來見禮。坐下細看時，真是與眾各別。只見兩彎籠(lǒng)煙眉，一雙含情目，淚光點點，嬌喘微微；閑靜似嬌花照水，行動如弱柳扶風。

寶玉看罷，笑道："這個妹妹我曾見過的。"賈母笑道："又胡說了，你何曾見過？"寶玉笑道："雖沒見過，卻看著面

---

① 賈母——黛玉的外祖母也被稱為賈母。

② 公子——古代對官員兒子的稱呼。

善,心裏倒像是遠別重逢的一般。"賈母笑道:"好,好!這就和睦了。"

寶玉便走向黛玉身邊坐下,又細細打量,因問:"妹妹可曾讀書?"黛玉道:"不曾讀書,只上了一年學,認得幾個字。"寶玉又道:"妹妹尊名?"黛玉便說了名,寶玉又問黛玉:"可有玉沒有?"黛玉想:"因他有玉,所以才問我的。"便答道:"我沒有玉。你那玉也是件稀罕物兒,哪能人人都有?"寶玉聽了,突然發作起狂病來,摘下那玉就狠命摔去,罵道:"什麼稀罕物!人的高下不識,還說靈不靈呢!我也不要了!"嚇得眾人一擁爭去拾玉。賈母急得摟了寶玉道:"你生氣要打罵人容易,何苦摔那命根子!"寶玉哭道:"家裏姐姐妹妹都沒有,單我有;如今來了這個天仙似的妹妹也沒有,可知這不是個好東西。"賈母忙哄他道:"你這妹妹原有玉來著。因你姑媽去世時,捨不得你妹妹,便把她的玉帶了去。"說著便從丫頭手中接過玉來親自給他帶上。寶玉聽了,信以為真,也就不再說什麼了。

(根據曹雪芹著《紅樓夢》第三回改編)

作品簡介

《紅樓夢》原名《石頭記》,是中國古代最優秀的長篇小說之一。作者曹雪芹(約1715—1763),清朝人。

《紅樓夢》一書共描寫了400多個人物,作品語言優美而有詩意,再現了當時社會生活的場景和細節。全書以賈寶玉、林黛玉、薛寶釵的愛情悲劇為主線,描寫了賈

家這個封建貴族大家庭衰亡的過程。寶玉反對男尊女卑、要求平等和個性解放；黛玉重愛情、輕功名，她和寶玉的愛情與這個封建家庭產生了矛盾。本課描寫了黛玉在外祖母家第一次見到寶玉的情景。

本文人物

賈寶玉：賈母的孫子，王夫人的兒子。
林黛玉：賈母的外孫女，寶玉的表妹。
王熙鳳：賈璉的妻子，寶玉的嫂子。
賈母：寶玉的奶奶，黛玉的姥姥。
王夫人：寶玉的母親，黛玉的舅媽。

生詞

dài yù 黛玉	Daiyu (name)	mó wáng 魔王	Prince of the Devils
jiào zi 轎子	sedan chair	zhí 侄	nephew
tái jiē 臺階	flight of steps	céng jīng 曾經	once; formerly
gū niang 姑娘	girl	nì ài 溺愛	spoil; pamper
lǒu 摟	embrace; hug	biǎo xiōng 表兄	cousin brother
yōng zhe 擁著	crowd around	jiù 舅	maternal uncle; mother's brother
cǎi xiù 彩綉	colorful embroidery	jiǎ 賈	Jia (surname)
liǔ 柳	willow	guān 冠	headgear; hat
sǎo zi 嫂子	sister-in-law	cái 裁	cut
ràng zhe 讓著	yield (to); humor	bó zi 脖子	neck

第十課

ǎo 襖	a Chinese-style coat	xī han 稀罕	rare
wēi 微	slightly; tiny	kuáng 狂	crazy; mad
hú shuō 胡說	talk nonsense	shuāi 摔	fling; throw
chóngféng 重逢	meet again	líng yàn 靈（驗）	(of a prediction, etc.) accurate; efficacious
hé mù 和睦	harmonious	hǒng 哄	coax

聽寫

姑娘　柳　臺階　曾經　頑皮　表兄　溺愛　狂　哄　微

稀罕　讓著　*舅　摔

比一比

橋（大橋）
轎（轎車）

娘 { 姑娘
　　　娘娘 }

摟（摟住）
樓（大樓）

嫂（嫂子）
搜（搜身）

苗 { 苗條
　　　樹苗 }

哄（哄人）
共（共同）

95

詞語運用

和睦

我們和鄰居們相處得很和睦,從來沒有吵過架,鬧過彆扭。

重逢

老朋友們久別重逢,激動極了,人人都有說不完的話。

曾經

我曾經讀過《花季雨季》,很喜歡這本書。

他在中國旅遊時曾經到過長城。

近義詞

狠命——拼命　　頑皮——調皮　　唸——讀

姑娘——女郎　　姥姥——外祖母

反義詞

和睦——爭鬥　　　　稀罕——常見

多音字

zhuó 著　　zhe 著　　zháo 著

zhuó 衣著　　zhe 等著　　zháo 著急

詞語解釋

打量——觀察（人的衣著、外貌）。

苗條——（婦女身材）細長、柔美。

安分——老實、守規矩。

信以為真——把假話當成真的。

姑媽——父親的姐妹。

去世——（成年人）死去。

娘——母親、媽媽。

Lesson Ten

Daiyu and Baoyu

(An optional lesson)

When Daiyu went ashore, a sedan chair sent from the Rong Mansion was waiting for her. She got in and entered the city. She could see and observe the busy streets through the sedan windows. After traveling for a few hours, she noticed two huge stone lions in front of a three-arched gate on the north side of the street. She had arrived at the Rong Mansion. Some maids, colorfully dressed, were sitting on the steps. On seeing Daiyu, they came forward to greet her, smiling as they announced, "Miss Lin is here!"

As Daiyu entered the room, a silver-haired old lady who was supported by two maids, came over to greet her. Daiyu knew she must be her grandmother and was about to kowtow to her when the old lady embraced her, exclaiming, "My dearest!" and began to cry. Daiyu too burst out sobbing and weeping. It was only after much persuasion from everyone that Daiyu was finally able to stop and pay respects to her grandmother.

A short while later, a sound of laughter was heard from the rear courtyard and a voice could be heard saying, "I am late in greeting our guest from afar." Daiyu heard this and thought, "How rude! Everybody else here is refined in manners. Who can this lady be? " A beautiful woman, with a group of women and maids crowding round her, entered from the rear room. She wore a splendid robe with colorful embroidery. The woman was stunning in appearance and had a slender figure, with almond shaped eyes and delicate eyebrows. Daiyu stood up quickly to greet her. Her cousins introduced her to the lady, saying, "This is Cousin Jia Lian's wife." Taking her hand and looking her up and down, Xifeng said with a smile, "There are genuine beauties in this world, and I see one with my own eyes today!" Then she went on to say, "How old are you? Have you been to school? What medicine are you taking now? Don't be homesick. Whatever you want to eat, whatever games you wish to play, just let me know. If anyone doesn't treat you well, feel free to tell me." Daiyu answered all her questions.

After tea break, Daiyu was taken to see Lady Wang. "Your three girl cousins are very good indeed. Later when you study or do needlework together, you'll find out how good they are in humoring you," Lady Wang said. "There's just one thing that worries me. My son is a devil in disguise. Today he's gone to the temple and isn't back yet. You'll know him when you see him this evening. You don't have to bother about him. None of your cousins dare provoke him." Daiyu had once heard her mother talk about her nephew who was born with a piece of luminescent jade in his mouth. Spoiled by his grandmother, he disliked studying and was so unruly that nobody could do anything with him. Upon hearing what Lady Wang just said, Daiyu knew that this was her cousin brother. She said with a smile, "Were you talking about my brother cousin who had a piece of jade in his mouth when he was born? When I was home, Mother often spoke of him. He's one year older than me and is known as Baoyu. I understand that he is on good terms with all the sister cousins although he may mischievous. Now that I am here, I would naturally be with my sister cousins. I wouldn't provoke him." Lady Wang smiled as she said, "I don't think you understand. He is used to getting along with females since his childhood. If the girls don't pay him any attention, he behaves himself. If they chat with him for a while longer, he would be too excited to control himself. So I would advise you not to bother much about him." Daiyu promised to bear it in mind.

Grandmother asked Daiyu what books she had studied. Daiyu replied, "I've just finished the Four Books." She wanted to know what books her sister cousins had studied. Grandmother said, "It's hard to say what books they have covered. They have just learned a few characters. That's all." Just then, footsteps were heard. Someone announced, "Baoyu is coming." Daiyu was wondering what sort of a person her brother cousin was. When he entered, she saw that he was a young man of a noble family. He wore a golden crown ornamented with precious stones and a red jacket embroidered with butterflies. His face was like the mid-autumn moon and his fair complexion might be compared to the flowers in early spring. His hair was as neatly done as if trimmed with scissors, his eyebrows were dark as if painted with black ink, and his eyes were as crystal clear as the water in a brook. A beautiful piece of jade hung round his neck. Daiyu was surprised when she saw the jade. She thought, "How strange! It looks so familiar to me. Have I seen it somewhere before?" Baoyu paid his respects to Grandmother who told him to go see his mother. When Baoyu returned again, he had changed into a bright red coat with patterns but wore the same piece of jade around his neck. He wore green satin trousers with floral designs and a pair of thick-soled scarlet shoes. His natural charm and temperament were obvious in his eyes and brows.

Smiling at Baoyu, Grandmother said, "Come over and introduce yourself to your sister cousin." In fact, Baoyu had already taken a quick look at her earlier, and guessed that she was the daughter of Mrs. Lin, his aunt. Hurriedly, he came over to say "Hi" to her. When he sat and looked closely at her, his impression of this cousin was that she was different from others. Her brows were delicately arched, and her sparkling eyes were filled with emotions and faint tenderness. When she was still, she looked like a tender flower reflected in a stream and when she moved, she was like the feeble willow dangling in the wind.

Baoyu said with a smile, "I've seen her before." Grandmother laughed and said, "There you go again with your nonsense. When did you see her?" He continued smiling and said, "Even though I haven't met her, she looks familiar. In my heart, it feels like we're meeting again after a long separation." Grandmother replied, "I'm glad to hear that! In that case, you'll get along harmoniously."

Baoyu walked over and sat beside Daiyu. He continued to scrutinize her. "Have you ever studied in school, sister?" he asked. To this, Daiyu replied, "Not really. I did go to school for one year though. All I learned there were a few characters." Baoyu asked again, "What is your name?" Daiyu told him her name. Baoyu put a third question to her, "Do you have a piece of jade with you?" Realizing that he was referring to the possession of a piece of jade like his own, she replied, "No, I haven't. Yours is a rare piece of jade. How can everyone possibly have one?" Her remarks made him mad all of a sudden. He took the jade off and threw it onto the ground, cursing, "What rare object! It can't distinguish what's superior from what's inferior. What spiritual nature does it have? I don't want to keep it any longer!" Everyone was so frightened that they rushed to pick the jade up. Grandmother quickly held Baoyu in her arms, saying, "You may beat or curse anyone if you're angry, but why throw away an object that is of such vital importance?" Baoyu cried as he said, "None of my sisters have one. I am the only member in the family who has it. Now my fairy-like sister doesn't have one either. Obviously, it is not a good thing." Grandmother coaxed him, saying, "Your younger sister did have one. But she gave it to her dying mother as a remembrance because her mother was so sad to have to part with her daughter." Then Grandmother took the jade from a maid, and put it round his neck again. Baoyu believed her story and said nothing more about it.

(Adapted from Chapter 3 of *Dream of the Red Chamber by Cao Xueqin*)

生字表（繁）

1. liáng gāng zuì hǒu shù chèn lūn jié jìn zhēng tī chuí quán
   梁 岡 醉 吼 豎 趁 掄 截 勁 掙 踢 錘 拳
   chì kǒng
   赤 恐

2. máng zhāo niǔ cā yān zhī biè wù shì zhuāng tán fēng tì chán fú
   茫 招 扭 擦 胭 脂 彆 務 飾 妝 談 封 替 纏 扶

3. zhū gě diāo fù zé cí dū gōng fèi qiān tuō yán lǔ
   諸 葛 刁 負 責 辭 督 攻 費 簽 拖 延 魯
   mì sī zhē bǎi fēn fù zhài gǔ dí réng sàn miào
   秘 私 遮 擺 吩 咐 寨 鼓 敵 仍 散 妙

4. wù sēng jiè yāo pú sà dǎi bàng lán suí shī bō è zhù
   悟 僧 戒 妖 菩 薩 歹 棒 攔 隨 屍 撥 惡 拄
   biàn háo fēng mú dāi qiǎo
   辯 毫 瘋 模 呆 巧

5. cūn tóng shào qiǎng bǎng biān sōu gù bǎo liū huàn tuō duō suō
   村 童 哨 搶 綁 鞭 搜 顧 飽 溜 喚 脫 哆 嗦
   fèng huī chà
   縫 揮 岔

6. wéi yì tiě ān jùn mù sù dàn fù ruò shuò cè xūn cì
   唯 亦 帖 鞍 駿 暮 宿 旦 赴 若 朔 策 勳 賜
   yù zǐ gé shang tiē huǒ bàn jiē huáng láng cí biàn
   欲 姊 閣 裳 貼 伙 伴 皆 惶 郎 雌 辨

7. shì bì qū pěng lóng diǎn bīn qiè dǐ kàng jī zhí bì
   氏 璧 屈 捧 隆 典 賓 怯 抵 抗 擊 職 避
   miǎn jīng xié
   免 荊 協

8. chén gǎo xí yú róu piān yǐ zhòu méi bì miáo dì shù
   陳 搞 襲 余 揉 偏 倚 皺 眉 弊 描 遞 束
   zé xíng shū wěi xiāo xū wěi jì jī shuài qiáo yǐn mán jùn
   擇 型 梳 委 蕭 虛 偽 績 激 帥 喬 隱 瞞 俊
   qiǎn jué
   淺 絕

101

9. 卧(wò) 賊(zéi) 遇(yù) 齡(líng) 益(yì) 臨(lín) 惹(rě) 塵(chén) 般(bān) 盯(dīng) 嘻(xī) 肩(jiān) 縮(suō) 衫(shān)
　　副(fù) 欺(qī) 惱(nǎo) 羞(xiū) 怒(nù) 輩(bèi) 敏(mǐn) 捷(jié) 腕(wàn) 紫(zǐ) 厭(yàn) 閑(xián)

10. 黛(dài) 轎(jiào) 階(jiē) 姑(gū) 摟(lǒu) 擁(yōng) 繡(xiù) 柳(liǔ) 嫂(sǎo) 魔(mó) 侄(zhí) 曾(céng) 溺(nì) 舅(jiù)
　　賈(jiǎ) 冠(guān) 裁(cái) 脖(bó) 襖(ǎo) 微(wēi) 逢(féng) 睦(mù) 罕(hǎn) 狂(kuáng) 摔(shuāi) 靈(líng) 哄(hǒng)

共計216個生字

生字表(简)

1. liáng gāng zuì hǒu shù chèn lūn jié jìn zhēng tī chuí quán
   梁 冈 醉 吼 竖 趁 抡 截 劲 挣 踢 锤 拳
   chì kǒng
   赤 恐

2. máng zhāo niǔ cā yān zhī bié wù shì zhuāng tán fēng tì chán fú
   茫 招 扭 擦 胭 脂 别 务 饰 妆 谈 封 替 缠 扶

3. zhū gě diāo fù zé cí dū gōng fèi qiān tuō yán lǔ
   诸 葛 刁 负 责 辞 督 攻 费 签 拖 延 鲁
   mì sī zhē bǎi fēn fù zhài gǔ dí réng sàn miào
   秘 私 遮 摆 吩 咐 寨 鼓 敌 仍 散 妙

4. wù sēng jiè yāo pú sà dǎi bàng lán suí shī bō è zhǔ
   悟 僧 戒 妖 菩 萨 歹 棒 拦 随 尸 拨 恶 拄
   biàn háo fēng mú dāi qiǎo
   辩 毫 疯 模 呆 巧

5. cūn tóng shào qiǎng bǎng biān sōu gù bǎo liū huàn tuō duō suō
   村 童 哨 抢 绑 鞭 搜 顾 饱 溜 唤 脱 哆 嗦
   fèng huī chà
   缝 挥 岔

6. wéi yì tiě ān jùn mù sù dàn fù ruò shuò cè xūn cì
   唯 亦 帖 鞍 骏 暮 宿 旦 赴 若 朔 策 勋 赐
   yù zǐ gé shang tiē huǒ bàn jiē huáng láng cí biàn
   欲 姊 阁 裳 贴 伙 伴 皆 惶 郎 雌 辨

7. shì bì qū pěng lóng diǎn bīn qiè dǐ kàng jī zhí bì
   氏 璧 屈 捧 隆 典 宾 怯 抵 抗 击 职 避
   miǎn jīng xié
   免 荆 协

8. chén gǎo xí yú róu piān yǐ zhòu méi bì miáo dì shù
   陈 搞 袭 余 揉 偏 倚 皱 眉 弊 描 递 束
   zé xíng shū wěi xiāo xū wěi jì jī shuài qiáo yǐn mán jùn
   择 型 梳 委 萧 虚 伪 绩 激 帅 乔 隐 瞒 俊
   qiǎn jué
   浅 绝

9. 卧(wò) 贼(zéi) 遇(yù) 龄(líng) 益(yì) 临(lín) 惹(rě) 尘(chén) 般(bān) 盯(dīng) 嘻(xī) 肩(jiān) 缩(suō) 衫(shān)
   副(fù) 欺(qī) 恼(nǎo) 羞(xiū) 怒(nù) 辈(bèi) 敏(mǐn) 捷(jié) 腕(wàn) 紫(zǐ) 厌(yàn) 闲(xián)

10. 黛(dài) 轿(jiào) 阶(jiē) 姑(gū) 搂(lǒu) 拥(yōng) 绣(xiù) 柳(liǔ) 嫂(sǎo) 魔(mó) 侄(zhí) 曾(céng) 溺(nì) 舅(jiù)
    贾(jiǎ) 冠(guān) 裁(cái) 脖(bó) 袄(ǎo) 微(wēi) 逢(féng) 睦(mù) 罕(hǎn) 狂(kuáng) 摔(shuāi) 灵(líng) 哄(hǒng)

共计216个生字

生詞表（繁）

1. liángshān 梁山　jiǔdiàn 酒店　jǐngyánggāng 景陽岡　zuì 醉　quàngào 勸告　bùgào 佈告　zhènghǎo 正好　hǒu 吼　shù 豎
chènzhe 趁著　lūn 掄　liǎng jié 兩截　shǐ jìn 使勁　zhēng zhá 掙扎　tī 踢　tiě chuí 鐵錘　quántou 拳頭
chì shǒu kōng quán 赤手空拳　zhēng xiān kǒng hòu 爭先恐後　shǎngqián 賞錢

2. jīngshāng 經商　mángmáng 茫茫　zuò mǎi mai 做買賣　lǎobǎn 老闆　zhāohu 招呼　shēncái 身材　niǔ nie 扭捏
cā yān zhi 擦胭脂　xī qí gǔ guài 稀奇古怪　biè niu 彆扭　guǎn lǐ 管理　jiā wù 家務　shǒu shi 首飾　huà zhuāng pǐn 化妝品
tán 談　fēng 封　tì 替　chán 纏　fú 扶　děi 得　āi qiú 哀求

3. cái zhì 才智　diāonàn 刁難　fù zé 負責　tuī cí 推辭　dū du 都督　jìn gōng 進攻　huā fèi 花費　kǒng pà 恐怕
wù shì 誤事　qiān zì 簽（字）　tuō yán 拖延　shuō dà huà 說大話　mì mì 秘密　sī zì 私自　zhē 遮　bǎi 擺
fēn fù 吩咐　shuǐzhài 水寨　qiāo gǔ 敲鼓　dí rén 敵人　mái fú 埋伏　réng jiù 仍舊　sàn qù 散去　shén jī miàosuàn 神機妙算

4. wù kōng 悟空　tángsēng 唐僧　jīn dǒu 筋斗　bā jiè 八戒　yāojing 妖精　yùn qi 運氣　pú sà 菩薩　tú di 徒弟　hǎo dǎi 好歹
bàng zi 棒子　lán zhù 攔住　suí biàn 隨便　jiǎ shī 假屍　tiǎo bō 挑撥　è 惡　zhǔ zhe 拄著　zhēngbiàn 爭辯　wéinán 為難
háomáo 毫毛　fā fēng 發瘋　múyàng 模樣　dāi zi 呆子　liú xīn 留心　qiǎo 巧

5. cūn zhuāng 村莊　ér tóng 兒童　fàngshào 放哨　jǐn jí 緊急　qiǎng 搶　miányáng 綿羊　bǎng 綁　biān zi 鞭子　sōu 搜
gù bu shàng 顧不上　chī bǎo 吃飽　liū 溜　jiàohuan 叫喚　tuō 脫　duō suo 哆嗦　fèng 縫　huī 揮　chōuyān 抽煙
chà lù 岔路　pīn mìng 拼命

中國文學欣賞

6. 唯(wéi) 亦(yì) 軍帖(jūn tiě) 鞍(ān) 駿馬(jùn mǎ) 暮宿(mù sù) 旦(dàn) 赴(fù) 若(ruò) 朔氣(shuò qì)
策勳(cè xūn) 賞賜(shǎng cì) 欲(yù) 姊(zǐ) 閣(gé) (衣)裳(yī shang) 貼(tiē) 伙伴(huǒ bàn) 皆(jiē)
驚惶(jīng huáng) 女郎(nǚ láng) 雌(cí) 辨(別)(biàn bié)

7. 和氏璧(hé shì bì) 機智(jī zhì) 理屈(lǐ qū) 捧著(pěng zhe) 稱讚(chēng zàn) 隆重(lóng zhòng) 約(yuē) 典禮(diǎn lǐ)
賓館(bīn guǎn) 大方(dà fang) 客氣(kè qì) 膽怯(dǎn qiè) 抵抗(dǐ kàng) 擊(jī) 佔便宜(zhàn pián yi) 職位(zhí wèi)
避免(bì miǎn) 諸位(zhū wèi) 荊條(jīng tiáo) 同心協力(tóng xīn xié lì)

8. 搞(gǎo) 襲擊(xí jī) 揉(róu) 不偏不倚(bù piān bù yǐ) 皺眉(zhòu méi) 作弊(zuò bì) 實際上(shí jì shang) 掃描(sǎo miáo)
遞(dì) 硬著頭皮(yìng zhe tóu pí) 及格(jí gé) 結束(jié shù) 選擇(xuǎn zé) 髮型(fà xíng) 梳頭(shū tóu) 委員(wěi yuán)
流行(liú xíng) 虛偽(xū wěi) 成績(chéng jì) 激動(jī dòng) 帥哥(shuài gē) 喬丹(qiáo dān) 興奮(xīng fèn) 隱瞞(yǐn mán)
英俊(yīng jùn) 淺(qiǎn) 絕對(jué duì)

9. 臥(wò) 馬賊(mǎ zéi) 遇(yù) 外號(wài hào) 年齡(nián líng) 老當益壯(lǎo dāng yì zhuàng) 臨行(lín xíng) 惹(rě) 塵沙(chén shā)
一般(yì bān) 作對(zuò duì) 盯(dīng) 打量(dǎ liang) 嘻皮笑臉(xī pí xiào liǎn) 肩(jiān) 縮(suō) 白布衫(bái bù shān)
一副(yí fù) 欺負(qī fu) 惱羞成怒(nǎo xiū chéng nù) 輩(bèi) 敏捷(mǐn jié) 手腕(shǒu wàn) 紫(zǐ) 厭惡(yàn wù) 閑事(xián shì)

10. 黛玉(dài yù) 轎子(jiào zi) 臺階(tái jiē) 姑娘(gū niang) 摟(lǒu) 擁著(yōng zhe) 彩綉(cǎi xiù) 柳(liǔ) 嫂子(sǎo zi)
讓著(ràng zhe) 魔王(mó wáng) 侄(zhí) 曾經(céng jīng) 溺愛(nì ài) 表兄(biǎo xiōng) 舅(jiù) 紫金冠(zǐ jīn guān) 裁(cái)
脖子(bó zi) 襖(ǎo) 微(wēi) 胡說(hú shuō) 重逢(chóng féng) 和睦(hé mù) 稀罕(xī han) 狂(kuáng) 摔(shuāi)
靈(驗)(líng yàn) 哄(hǒng)

共計235個生詞

生词表（简）

1. 梁山(liángshān) 酒店(jiǔdiàn) 景阳冈(jǐngyánggāng) 醉(zuì) 劝告(quàngào) 布告(bùgào) 正好(zhènghǎo) 吼(hǒu) 竖(shù) 趁著(chènzhe) 抡(lūn) 两截(liǎng jié) 使劲(shǐ jìn) 挣扎(zhēng zhá) 踢(tī) 铁锤(tiě chuí) 拳头(quántou) 赤手空拳(chì shǒu kōng quán) 争先恐后(zhēng xiān kǒng hòu) 赏钱(shǎng qián)

2. 经商(jīngshāng) 茫茫(mángmáng) 做买卖(zuò mǎimai) 老板(lǎobǎn) 招呼(zhāohu) 身材(shēncái) 扭捏(niǔnie) 擦胭脂(cā yānzhi) 稀奇古怪(xī qí gǔ guài) 别扭(bièniu) 管理(guǎnlǐ) 家务(jiāwù) 首饰(shǒushi) 化妆品(huàzhuāngpǐn) 谈(tán) 封(fēng) 替(tì) 缠(chán) 扶(fú) 得(děi) 哀求(āiqiú)

3. 才智(cáizhì) 刁难(diāonàn) 负责(fùzé) 推辞(tuīcí) 都督(dūdu) 进攻(jìngōng) 花费(huāfèi) 恐怕(kǒngpà) 误事(wùshì) 签(字)(qiān zì) 拖延(tuōyán) 说大话(shuō dà huà) 秘密(mìmì) 私自(sīzì) 遮(zhē) 摆(bǎi) 吩咐(fēnfù) 水寨(shuǐzhài) 敲鼓(qiāogǔ) 敌人(dírén) 埋伏(máifú) 仍旧(réngjiù) 散去(sànqù) 神机妙算(shén jī miàosuàn)

4. 悟空(wùkōng) 唐僧(tángsēng) 筋斗(jīndǒu) 八戒(bājiè) 妖精(yāojing) 运气(yùnqi) 菩萨(púsà) 徒弟(túdi) 好歹(hǎodǎi) 棒子(bàngzi) 拦住(lánzhù) 随便(suíbiàn) 假尸(jiǎ shī) 挑拨(tiǎobō) 恶(è) 拄著(zhǔzhe) 争辩(zhēngbiàn) 为难(wéinán) 毫毛(háomáo) 发疯(fāfēng) 模样(múyàng) 呆子(dāizi) 留心(liúxīn) 巧(qiǎo)

5. 村庄(cūnzhuāng) 儿童(értóng) 放哨(fàngshào) 紧急(jǐnjí) 抢(qiǎng) 绵羊(miányáng) 绑(bǎng) 鞭子(biānzi) 搜(sōu) 顾不上(gù bu shàng) 吃饱(chī bǎo) 溜(liū) 叫唤(jiàohuan) 脱(tuō) 哆嗦(duōsuo) 缝(féng) 挥(huī) 抽烟(chōuyān) 岔路(chà lù) 拼命(pīnmìng)

107

中國文學欣賞

6. 唯(wéi) 亦(yì) 軍帖(jūn tiě) 鞍(ān) 駿馬(jùn mǎ) 暮宿(mù sù) 旦(dàn) 赴(fù) 若(ruò) 朔氣(shuò qì)
策勛(cè xūn) 賞賜(shǎng cì) 欲(yù) 姊(zǐ) 閣(gé) (衣)裳(yīshang) 貼(tiē) 伙伴(huǒbàn) 皆(jiē)
驚惶(jīng huáng) 女郎(nǚ láng) 雌(cí) 辨(biàn)（別(bié)）

7. 和氏璧(hé shì bì) 機智(jī zhì) 理屈(lǐ qū) 捧著(pěngzhe) 稱讚(chēng zàn) 隆重(lóngzhòng) 約(yuē) 典禮(diǎn lǐ)
賓館(bīnguǎn) 大方(dà fang) 客氣(kè qi) 膽怯(dǎn qiè) 抵抗(dǐ kàng) 擊(jī) 佔便宜(zhànpián yi) 職位(zhí wèi)
避免(bì miǎn) 諸位(zhū wèi) 荊條(jīngtiáo) 同心協力(tóng xīn xié lì)

8. 搞(gǎo) 襲擊(xí jī) 揉(róu) 不偏不倚(bù piān bù yǐ) 皺眉(zhòuméi) 作弊(zuò bì) 實際上(shí jì shang) 掃描(sǎomiáo)
遞(dì) 硬著頭皮(yìngzhe tóu pí) 及格(jí gé) 結束(jié shù) 選擇(xuǎn zé) 髮型(fà xíng) 梳頭(shū tóu) 委員(wěi yuán)
流行(liú xíng) 虛偽(xū wěi) 成績(chéng jì) 激動(jī dòng) 帥哥(shuài gē) 喬丹(qiáodān) 興奮(xīng fèn) 隱瞞(yǐn mán)
英俊(yīng jùn) 淺(qiǎn) 絕對(jué duì)

9. 臥(wò) 馬賊(mǎ zéi) 遇(yù) 外號(wàihào) 年齡(niánlíng) 老當益壯(lǎo dāng yì zhuàng) 臨行(lín xíng) 惹(rě) 塵沙(chénshā)
一般(yì bān) 作對(zuò duì) 盯(dīng) 打量(dǎ liang) 嬉皮笑臉(xī pí xiàoliǎn) 肩(jiān) 縮(suō) 白布衫(bái bù shān)
一副(yí fù) 欺負(qī fu) 惱羞成怒(nǎo xiū chéng nù) 輩(bèi) 敏捷(mǐn jié) 手腕(shǒuwàn) 紫(zǐ) 厭惡(yàn wù) 閒事(xián shì)

10. 黛玉(dài yù) 轎子(jiào zi) 台階(tái jiē) 姑娘(gū niang) 摟(lǒu) 擁著(yōngzhe) 彩繡(cǎi xiù) 柳(liǔ) 嫂子(sǎo zi)
讓著(ràngzhe) 魔王(mó wáng) 侄(zhí) 曾經(céngjīng) 溺愛(nì ài) 表兄(biǎoxiōng) 舅(jiù) 紫金冠(zǐ jīn guān) 裁(cái)
脖子(bó zi) 襖(ǎo) 微(wēi) 胡說(hú shuō) 重逢(chóng féng) 和睦(hé mù) 稀罕(xī han) 狂(kuáng) 摔(shuāi)
靈(líng)（驗(yàn)） 哄(hǒng)

共計235個生詞

第二課

一　寫生詞

茫	茫										
招	呼										
扭	捏										
擦											
胭	脂										
彆	扭										
家	務										
首	飾										
化	妝	品									
談											
封											
替											

纏											
扶											

二　組詞

扭＿＿　　擦＿＿　　胭＿＿　　茫＿＿

妝＿＿　　扶＿＿　　招＿＿　　務＿＿

飾＿＿　　談＿＿　　封＿＿　　替＿＿

三　選字組詞

美（丑　扭）　　（因　胭）為　　農（夫　扶）

彆（丑　扭）　　（因　胭）脂　　（夫　扶）著

（信　言）封　　化（妝　裝）品　　身（材　才）

語（信　言）　　服（妝　裝）　　（材　才）能

四　寫出反義詞

矮小——　　　　　　扭捏——

五 寫出多音字的拼音

1. 我用針在紙上扎（　　）了一個小孔。

2. 老虎被按在地上，雖然使勁挣扎（　　），但就是起不來。

六 根據課文選詞填空（把詞語寫在空白處）

細聲細氣　　胭脂　　彆扭

扭扭捏捏　　封　　不由分說　　纏足

1. 女兒國裏的男人穿著女人的衣服。他們臉上長著鬍子，可是走起路來＿＿＿＿＿＿的，說話也＿＿＿＿＿＿的，臉上還擦著香粉和＿＿＿＿＿＿呢！唐敖他們覺得＿＿＿＿＿＿極了。

2. 女國王一見到他們，就看上了林之洋，＿＿＿＿＿＿就＿＿＿＿＿＿了林之洋做"娘娘"。於是，宮"女"們拿來布條給林之洋＿＿＿＿＿＿。

七 選擇填空（把詞語寫在空白處）

　　1. 珠寶店裏有許多_____。（首飾　首都）

　　2. 小明的爸爸是商人，他_____出差。（經常　經過）

　　3. 昨天打球我不小心把腳_____了。（彆扭　扭傷）

八 根據課文判斷對錯

　　1. 在女兒國，女人掌管國家大事。　　　　　　　___對___錯

　　2. 在女兒國，男人戴花、擦胭脂，做家務。　　　___對___錯

　　3. 女國王要讓林之洋做"娘娘"。　　　　　　　　___對___錯

　　4. 林之洋被纏了足、扎了耳朵眼兒。　　　　　　___對___錯

　　5. 林之洋從來沒受過這麼多苦。　　　　　　　　___對___錯

　　6. 在女兒國裏，男人沒有地位。　　　　　　　　___對___錯

　　7. 林之洋他們不喜歡女兒國，逃跑了。　　　　　___對___錯

九 縮寫課文《女兒國》（至少寫十句話，必須使用下列詞語：經商、扭捏、談、化妝品、不由分說、封、纏足）

十 熟讀課文

第四課

一 寫生詞

悟	空										
唐	僧										
八	戒										
妖	精										
菩	薩										
好	歹										
棒	子										
攔	住										
隨	便										
假	屍										
挑	撥										
惡											

拄	著									
爭	辯									
毫	毛									
發	瘋									
模	樣									
呆	子									
巧										

二 組詞

悟＿＿＿　戒＿＿＿　妖＿＿＿　菩＿＿＿

歹＿＿＿　模＿＿＿　瘋＿＿＿　屍＿＿＿

撥＿＿＿　拄＿＿＿　呆＿＿＿　辯＿＿＿

棒＿＿＿　毫＿＿＿　攔＿＿＿　隨＿＿＿

三 選字組詞

（屋 屍）體　（拄 柱）著　（模 漠）樣　挑（撥 潑）

（屋 屍）子　（拄 柱）子　沙（模 漠）　活（撥 潑）

四 寫出反義詞

歹——　　　　善——　　　　舉起——

笨——　　　　鬆——

五 根據課文判斷對錯

1. 唐僧師徒四人去西天取經。　　　　　___對___錯

2. 妖精聽說吃了唐僧肉就能長生不老。　　___對___錯

3. 唐僧、八戒和沙僧都沒認出白骨精。　　___對___錯

4. 豬八戒總是跟師父說孫悟空的好話。　　___對___錯

5. 孫悟空不怕妖精,就怕師父唸緊箍咒(gū zhòu)。　___對___錯

6. 唐僧聽信了八戒的挑撥,把悟空趕走了。　___對___錯

7. 孫悟空三打白骨精都是為了保護師父。　　___對___錯

六 造句

1. 隨便_____

2. 埋怨_____

3. 舉_____

七 把解釋和相應的詞語連起來

咬緊牙，表示痛恨　　　　　　　回心轉意

不知道好壞　　　　　　　　　　咬牙切齒

改變主意，又回到原來的想法　　花言巧語

用好聽的話騙人　　　　　　　　不知好歹

八 回答問題

1. 《西遊記》的作者是誰？（生字可以寫漢語拼音）

　　答：_____

2. 唐僧師徒四人是哪四個人？

　　答：_____

3. 孫悟空有哪些本領？

　　答：_____

4. 豬八戒有哪些毛病？

　　答：_____

5. 美猴王是誰？

答：_____

6. 唐僧是不是很糊塗？

答：_____
_____

九 縮寫孫悟空第一次打白骨精的故事（至少寫十句話）

第六課

一 寫生詞

唯												
亦												
軍	帖											
鞍												
駿	馬											
暮												
宿												
旦												
赴												
若												
朔	氣											
策	勳											

賞賜											
欲											
姊											
閣											
衣裳											
貼											
伙伴											
皆											
驚惶											
女郎											
雌											
辨別											

二　組詞

唯_____　　帖_____　　駿_____　　賜_____

伙_____　　策_____　　旦_____　　貼_____

郎_____　　裳_____　　辨_____　　惶_____

三　選字組詞

　　回（憶　憶）　　　記（憶　憶）　　　考（圈　卷）

　　奔（起　赴）　　　賞（易　賜）　　　衣（裳　賞）

　　爭（辨　辯）　　　容（賜　易）　　　痛（苦　若）

四　寫出反義詞

　　暮──　　　　　貼──　　　　　歸來──

　　賞──

五　寫出下列詩句的意思

　　可汗問所欲，"木蘭不用尚書郎，
　　願借千里足，送兒還故鄉。"

　　_____

　　_____

　　脫我戰時袍，著我舊時裳。

　　當窗理雲鬢（bìn），對鏡貼花黃。

　　出門看伙伴，伙伴皆驚惶。

　　同行十二年，不知木蘭是女郎。

六 把《木蘭辭》改寫成一篇短文(至少寫十句話)

七 背誦《木蘭辭》

第八課

一　寫生詞

陳												
搞												
襲	擊											
余												
揉												
皺	眉											
作	弊											
掃	描											
遞												
結	束											
選	擇											
髮	型											

梳	頭											
委	員											
蕭												
虛	偽											
成	績											
激	動											
帥	哥											
喬												
隱	瞞											
英	俊											
淺												
絕	對											
不	偏	不	倚									

二　組詞

襲_____　　揉_____　　眉_____　　弊_____

束_____　　遞_____　　選_____　　描_____

績_____　　梳_____　　激_____　　俊_____

帥_____　　瞞_____　　隱_____　　委_____

型_____　　淺_____　　絕_____　　偏_____

三　選字組詞

（屋　握）拳　　　喝（彩　採）　　　（柔　揉）和

（屋　握）子　　　雲（彩　採）　　　（柔　揉）成團

（真　填）寫　　　虛（為　偽）　　　（退　腿）步

（真　填）假　　　（為　偽）了　　　四條（退　腿）

四　寫出反義詞

秘密——　　　　光榮——　　　　激動——

進步——　　　　抓緊——　　　　深——

五 根據課文選詞填空（把詞語寫在空白處）

教語文的　救兵　滿滿當當　學習委員
高一(4)班　王笑天　蕭遙

1. 陳老師是_____。

2. 事情發生在_____。

3. 陳老師出的卷子總是_____的。

4. 余發考試時想到的_____是王笑天。

5. 陳明是這個班裏的_____。

6. "小帥哥"是_____。

7. _____是高一(4)班的班長。

六 詞語解釋

1. 喝彩——

2. 帥哥——

3. 若有所思——

七 相配詞連線

　　　　　流行　　　　聽講
　　　　　用心　　　　時間
　　　　　抓緊　　　　音樂

八 根據課文寫一寫下列人物的情況（請寫一兩句話）

1. 陳老師 _____

_____

2. 余發 _____

_____

3. 王笑天 _____

_____

4. 陳明 _____

_____

九　回答問題

1. 你認為余發學習好不好？請從課文中找出你的根據來。

答：＿＿＿＿＿＿＿＿＿＿＿＿＿＿＿＿＿＿＿＿

＿＿＿＿＿＿＿＿＿＿＿＿＿＿＿＿＿＿＿＿＿＿

＿＿＿＿＿＿＿＿＿＿＿＿＿＿＿＿＿＿＿＿＿＿

2. 很多女生心目中的"白馬王子"是誰？

答：＿＿＿＿＿＿＿＿＿＿＿＿＿＿＿＿＿＿＿＿

＿＿＿＿＿＿＿＿＿＿＿＿＿＿＿＿＿＿＿＿＿＿

＿＿＿＿＿＿＿＿＿＿＿＿＿＿＿＿＿＿＿＿＿＿

3. 欣然認為男孩子光是英俊是不行的，還要有能力、有才氣、性格好。你的觀點呢？

答：＿＿＿＿＿＿＿＿＿＿＿＿＿＿＿＿＿＿＿＿

＿＿＿＿＿＿＿＿＿＿＿＿＿＿＿＿＿＿＿＿＿＿

＿＿＿＿＿＿＿＿＿＿＿＿＿＿＿＿＿＿＿＿＿＿

十　熟讀課文

第十課

一 寫生詞

黛	玉											
轎	子											
臺	階											
姑	娘											
摟												
擁	著											
彩	綉											
柳												
嫂	子											
魔	王											
侄												
曾	經											
溺	愛											

舅舅
貫
紫金冠
裁
脖子
襖
微
重逢
和睦
稀罕
狂
摔
靈驗
哄

二 組詞

姑_____　轎_____　綉_____　柳_____

舅_____　摔_____　魔_____　溺_____

逢_____　睦_____　罕_____　曾_____

侄_____　階_____　微_____　冠_____

三 選字組詞

大（橋　轎）　　臺（介　階）　　（共　哄）人

（橋　轎）車　　（介　階）紹　　（共　哄）同

四 寫出反義詞

和睦——　　　　　　稀罕——

五 選詞填空（把詞語寫在空白處）

賈寶玉　林黛玉　曹雪芹(qín)

1.《紅樓夢》的作者是_____。

2.《紅樓夢》的兩個主要人物是_____和_____。

六 把解釋和相應的詞語連起來

母親　　　　　　　　　　　　　信以為真

婦女身材細長柔美　　　　　　　打量

觀察（人的衣著外貌）　　　　　苗條

把假話當成真的　　　　　　　　娘

七 請回答各題中被描寫的人物是誰（生字可以用漢語拼音代替）

1. 這個人衣著彩綉輝煌，美若天仙；一雙丹鳳眼，兩彎柳葉眉，身材苗條。

答：她是＿＿＿＿＿＿＿＿

2. 頭戴寶石紫金冠；面若中秋之月，色如春曉之花，鬢(bìn)若刀裁，眉如墨畫，睛若秋波；脖子上掛著一塊美玉。

答：他是＿＿＿＿＿＿＿＿

3. 兩彎籠(lǒng)煙眉，一雙含情目，淚光點點，嬌喘微微；閑靜似嬌花照水，行動如弱柳扶風。

答：她是＿＿＿＿＿＿＿＿

第二課聽寫

第四課聽寫

第六課聽寫

第八課聽寫

第十課聽寫

第一課

一 寫生詞

梁	山										
岡											
醉											
吼											
豎											
趁	著										
掄											
兩	截										
使	勁										
掙	扎										
踢											
鐵	錘										
拳	頭										

赤	手	空	拳							
爭	先	恐	後							

二 組詞

梁＿＿＿＿　　截＿＿＿＿　　趁＿＿＿＿　　岡＿＿＿＿

踢＿＿＿＿　　豎＿＿＿＿　　掄＿＿＿＿　　錘＿＿＿＿

拳＿＿＿＿　　賞＿＿＿＿　　勁＿＿＿＿　　吼＿＿＿＿

掙＿＿＿＿　　赤＿＿＿＿　　爭＿＿＿＿

三 選字組詞

容（易　踢）　　　　　　　鬥（掙　爭）

（易　踢）球　　　　　　　（掙　爭）扎

車（輪　掄）　　　　　　　鐵（錘　睡）

（輪　掄）錘　　　　　　　（錘　睡）覺

四 寫出反義詞

使勁——　　　　　　橫——

五 選擇填空（把詞語寫在空白處）

1. 店家說：「這種酒叫做'三碗不過岡'，意思是說，人喝了三_____之后就會醉倒。」（杯　瓶　碗）

2. 武松聽了哈哈大笑，說：「我喝酒是海量，從來沒_____。」（暈過　哭過　醉過）

3. 武松不聽店家的勸告，提著一根_____就上山去了。（繩子　棍子　竹子）

4. 老虎氣得大_____一聲。（吼　孔）

5. 姐姐_____古典音樂，而我喜歡搖滾樂。

（賞錢　欣賞）

6. 每個星期六弟弟都去_____足球。（踢　易）

7. 對我來說，說中文比寫中文更容_____。（易　踢）

六 根據課文選詞填空（把詞語寫在空白處）

亂抓　拳頭　使勁　坑　漸漸

老虎被武松緊緊地按在地上，就用兩隻爪子在地上_____，把地挖出了一個____。老虎_____沒有力氣了。武松掄起鐵錘般的_____，照著老虎的頭_____地打。

七 根據課文判斷對錯

1. 武松是一位梁山好漢,打虎英雄。　　　　　＿＿對＿＿錯

2. 武松不怕老虎,因為他覺得自己有棍子。　　＿＿對＿＿錯

3. 武松看見官府的佈告,纔知道真的有老虎。

　　　　　　　　　　　　　　　　　　　　　＿＿對＿＿錯

4. 武松喝醉了酒,看見一塊空地,就往地
   上一躺睡了。　　　　　　　　　　　　　　＿＿對＿＿錯

5. 老虎的吼聲像打雷。　　　　　　　　　　　＿＿對＿＿錯

6. 武松用棍子打死了老虎。　　　　　　　　　＿＿對＿＿錯

7. 武松的拳頭像鐵錘,很有勁。　　　　　　　＿＿對＿＿錯

8. 武松把賞錢買酒喝了。　　　　　　　　　　＿＿對＿＿錯

9. "武松打虎"是小說《水滸(hǔ)傳》中的故事。　＿＿對＿＿錯

八 造句

1. 趁著＿＿＿＿＿＿＿＿＿＿＿＿＿＿＿＿＿＿＿＿＿

2. 爭先恐後＿＿＿＿＿＿＿＿＿＿＿＿＿＿＿＿＿＿＿

3. 使勁＿＿＿＿＿＿＿＿＿＿＿＿＿＿＿＿＿＿＿＿＿

九　縮寫課文《武松打虎》（至少寫十句話，必須使用下列詞語：梁山好漢、酒店、佈告、亂踢、掄起拳頭、使勁、赤手空拳）

十　熟讀課文

第三課

一　寫生詞

諸葛										
刁難										
負責										
推辭										
都督										
進攻										
花費										
簽字										
拖延										
魯										
秘密										
私自										

遮												
擺												
吩	咐											
水	寨											
敲	鼓											
敵	人											
仍	舊											
散	去											
神	機	妙	算									

二 組詞

刁_____　　負_____　　推_____　　攻_____

拖_____　　敵_____　　仍_____　　鼓_____

埋_____　　吩_____　　私_____　　秘_____

擺_____　　費_____　　妙_____　　散_____

三 選字組詞

（叼　刁）難　　　誤（是　事）　　　幸（福　幅）

（射　謝）箭　　　仍（歸　舊）　　　（吩　份）咐

四 選擇填空

1. "草船借箭"是長篇歷史小説_____^{piān}中的故事。

（《三國演義》　《西遊記》^{yì}　《紅樓夢》）

2. 《三國演義》是一部中國古代優秀的_____。

（長篇歷史小説　神話故事）

3. 《三國演義》的作者是_____。

（施耐庵^{shī ān}　羅貫中^{guàn}）

五 根據課文判斷對錯

1. 周瑜才智過人，諸葛亮總是刁難他。　　____對____錯

2. 水陸交戰，諸葛亮和周瑜都認為使用
   弓箭最好。　　　　　　　　　　　　　　____對____錯

3. 諸葛亮滿口答應三天之內造十萬支箭

給周瑜。　　　　　　　　　　　　＿＿對＿＿錯

4. 諸葛亮表示三天造不出十萬支箭願受重罰。　　　　　　　　　　　　＿＿對＿＿錯

5. 魯肅是周瑜的手下，也是諸葛亮的好朋友。　　　　　　　　　　　　＿＿對＿＿錯

6. 魯肅背著周瑜幫諸葛亮的忙。　＿＿對＿＿錯

7. 諸葛亮吩咐把二十條船一個接一個地用繩子連接起來。　　　　　　　　＿＿對＿＿錯

8. 江上下起了大雪，江面上什麼都看不清。＿＿對＿＿錯

9. 諸葛亮叫船上的士兵敲鼓大喊，他和魯肅在船裏喝酒。　　　　　　　　＿＿對＿＿錯

10. 曹軍向江裏放箭，箭好像下雨一樣。＿＿對＿＿錯

11. 諸葛亮只用了三天就取得了十萬多支箭。　　　　　　　　　　　　＿＿對＿＿錯

六　造句

1. 秘密＿＿＿＿＿＿＿＿＿＿＿＿＿＿＿＿
2. 恐怕＿＿＿＿＿＿＿＿＿＿＿＿＿＿＿＿
3. 仍舊＿＿＿＿＿＿＿＿＿＿＿＿＿＿＿＿

七 根據課文回答問題

1. 周瑜是怎樣刁難諸葛亮的？

   答：_____

   _____

   _____

2. 諸葛亮請魯肅幫他做什麼？

   答：_____

   _____

   _____

3. 諸葛亮用什麼辦法三天造出了十萬支箭？

   答：_____

   _____

   _____

   _____

八　縮寫課文《草船借箭》（至少寫十句話，必須使用下列詞語：負責、推辭、恐怕、簽、拖延、私自、神機妙算）

九　熟讀課文

第五課

一 寫生詞

村	莊										
兒	童										
放	哨										
搶											
綁											
鞭	子										
搜											
顧	不	上									
吃	飽										
溜											
叫	喚										
脫											

哆	嗦											
縫												
揮												
岔	路											

二　組詞

村_____　　童_____　　鞭_____　　搶_____

拼_____　　搜_____　　脫_____　　飽_____

縫_____　　溜_____　　哨_____　　揮_____

喚_____　　顧_____

三　選字組詞

（寸　村）莊　　兒（撞　童）　　（採　踩）雷

尺（村　寸）　　（童　撞）倒　　（踩　採）花

（搶　槍）糧　　吃（包　飽）　　（拼　併）命

手（搶　槍）　　書（飽　包）　　合（拼　併）

（溜　留）走　　　叫（換　喚）　　　（傍　旁）邊

（溜　留）下　　　（換　喚）衣　　　（旁　傍）晚

四　寫出反義詞

擔心—— 　　　　飽—— 　　　　傍晚——

綁上—— 　　　　脫—— 　　　　歪——

五　根據課文選擇填空

1. 海娃聽出是爸爸的聲音，連忙_____。

（跑走　迎上去）

2. 信上插著三根雞毛，海娃知道是一封很_____信。

（緊急的　平常的）

六　根據課文判斷對錯

1. 海娃十四歲，是龍門市兒童團的團長。　　___對___錯

2. 爸爸讓海娃把一封信送給張隊長。　　　　___對___錯

3. 海娃接過信一看，信上插著三根鴨毛。　　___對___錯

4. 送信的路上，海娃碰見了一隊搶糧的

　　日本兵。　　　　　　　　　　　　　　___對___錯

5. 海娃著急了,把雞毛信藏在老山羊的
   尾巴底下。　　　　　　　　　　　　　___對___錯

6. 日本兵宰了幾隻海娃的羊,燒羊肉吃了。　___對___錯

7. 海娃脫下白上衣,也來回搖晃,把信丟了。　___對___錯

8. 日本兵讓海娃帶路,海娃把他們帶上了
   羊走的小道。　　　　　　　　　　　　___對___錯

9. 海娃是個小英雄!　　　　　　　　　　___對___錯

七 造句

1. 傍晚_____
2. 村莊_____
3. 拼命_____

八 詞語解釋

1. 趕緊——
2. 心疼——
3. 顧不上——

九 短文擴寫

例：{ 海娃跑到山頂。　　　　{ 他坐在山頭上。
    { 海娃一口氣跑到山頂。　{ 他一屁股坐在山頭上。

海娃跑到山頂。前面就是王莊啦,海娃高興極了。他坐在山頭上,把手伸進口袋一摸,雞毛信呢?口袋裏沒有,上衣也沒有。海娃馬上往回跑,在來的路上找。他爬上山,就在剛才搖晃衣服的地方,雞毛信躺在那兒。

十 熟讀課文

第七課

一 寫生詞

和	氏	璧									
理	屈										
捧	著										
隆	重										
典	禮										
賓	館										
膽	怯										
抵	抗										
擊											
職	位										
避	免										
荊	條										

同	心	協	力								

二 組詞

氏＿＿＿　　荊＿＿＿　　屈＿＿＿　　捧＿＿＿

隆＿＿＿　　典＿＿＿　　賓＿＿＿　　怯＿＿＿

抵＿＿＿　　抗＿＿＿　　職＿＿＿　　避＿＿＿

免＿＿＿　　協＿＿＿

三 選字組詞

（辟　避）開　　（璧　壁）玉　　賓（官　館）

開（辟　避）　　牆（璧　壁）　　（官　館）員

（捧　棒）著　　（兔　免）子　　抵（坑　抗）

（捧　棒）子　　（兔　免）得　　挖（坑　抗）

四 寫出反義詞

進攻——　　　膽怯——　　　吃虧——

五 選擇填空

1.《將相和》是_____中的故事。

　　　　　　　　　　　　　　（《史記》 《西遊記》）

2.《史記》的作者是_____。（司馬遷(qiān)　羅貫(guàn)中）

六 根據課文判斷對錯

1. 戰國時候，秦國兵力不強。　　　　　　　　　___對___錯

2. 趙王得了一塊寶玉叫"和氏璧"。　　　　　　 ___對___錯

3. 秦王想要這塊寶玉。　　　　　　　　　　　　___對___錯

4. 趙王不想把寶玉給秦王，可又害怕秦王。　　 ___對___錯

5. 藺(lìn)相如看出秦王是騙子。　　　　　　　　___對___錯

6. 藺相如比秦王聰明。　　　　　　　　　　　　___對___錯

7. 藺相如的職位比廉頗(lián pō)高，廉頗不服氣。___對___錯

8. 藺相如很有勇氣，不怕秦王。　　　　　　　　___對___錯

9. 廉頗脫下戰袍，背上荊條，到藺相如府

　 上請罪。　　　　　　　　　　　　　　　　　___對___錯

10. 廉頗和藺相如最后成了好朋友，同心協力保衛趙國。　　　　　　　　　＿＿對＿＿錯

七　造句

例句：我們出去旅遊，住在一家四星級賓館裏。

學校的開學典禮很隆重。

由於哥哥會講中文，他得到了一個好職位。

1. 賓館＿＿＿＿＿＿＿＿＿＿＿＿＿＿＿＿＿＿
2. 典禮＿＿＿＿＿＿＿＿＿＿＿＿＿＿＿＿＿＿
3. 職位＿＿＿＿＿＿＿＿＿＿＿＿＿＿＿＿＿＿

八　相配詞連線

維護　　　　問題

舉行　　　　國家

解決　　　　利益

保衛　　　　典禮

九　縮寫課文《將相和》（至少寫十句話，必須使用下列詞語：商議、理由、捧著、隆重、典禮、職位、避免、負荊請罪）

十　熟讀課文

第九課

一 寫生詞

卧											
賊											
遇											
年	齡										
老	當	益	壯								
臨	行										
惹											
塵	沙										
一	般										
盯											
嘻	皮	笑	臉								
肩											
縮											

白	布	衫									
一	副										
欺	負										
輩											
敏	捷										
手	腕										
紫											
厭	惡										
閒	事										
惱	羞	成	怒								

二 組詞

厭＿＿＿＿　閒＿＿＿＿　紫＿＿＿＿　齡＿＿＿＿

臨＿＿＿＿　縮＿＿＿＿　欺＿＿＿＿　塵＿＿＿＿

衫＿＿＿＿　惱＿＿＿＿　輩＿＿＿＿　捷＿＿＿＿

腕＿＿＿＿　縮＿＿＿＿　副＿＿＿＿　般＿＿＿＿

遇＿＿＿＿　盯＿＿＿＿　怒＿＿＿＿　益＿＿＿＿

三 選字組詞

（腰　要）帶　　　（盯　釘）著　　　（欺　期）負

彎（腰　要）　　　（盯　釘）木板　　　星（欺　期）

四 近義詞連線

賊　　　　　　勇敢

相貌　　　　　討厭

勇猛　　　　　面容

年齡　　　　　碰到

遇到　　　　　小偷

厭惡　　　　　年歲

五 寫出反義詞

伸——　　　　　　欺負——

閒——　　　　　　厭惡——

六 根據課文判斷對錯

1. 領頭的馬賊外號叫半天雲。　　　＿＿對＿＿錯

2. 這半天雲很厲害。　　　　　　　＿＿對＿＿錯

3. 馬賊專門和官家、地主、頭人作對。＿＿對＿＿錯

4. 巴格想欺負玉小姐。　　　　　　＿＿對＿＿錯

5. 巴格咬了玉小姐的手。　　　　　＿＿對＿＿錯

6. 有個漢子救了玉小姐。　　　　　＿＿對＿＿錯

七 造句

1. 敏捷＿＿＿＿＿＿＿＿＿＿＿＿＿＿＿＿＿＿＿

2. 欺負＿＿＿＿＿＿＿＿＿＿＿＿＿＿＿＿＿＿＿

八 詞語解釋

1. 紋絲不動——

2. 一表人才——

3. 老當益壯——

4. 留神——

九　縮寫課文《卧虎藏龍》（至少寫十句話）

十　熟讀課文

第一課聽寫

第三課聽寫

第五課聽寫

第七課聽寫

第九課聽寫

練習紙

中國文學欣賞

練習紙